ASPIRATIONS FOR IRELAND

Edited by Susannah Kingston

Aspirations for Ireland

NEW WAYS FORWARD

the columba press

First published in 2010 by
the columba press
55A Spruce Avenue, Stillorgan Industrial Park,
Blackrock, Co Dublin

Cover by Bill Bolger
Origination by The Columba Press
Printed in Ireland by ColourBooks Ltd, Dublin

ISBN 978 1 85607 720 0

Acknowledgements

I would like to express my sincere thanks to Mary and Billy Kingston, Edward Redding, Suzanne Connolly, John Feehan, Christina Cassidy, Paula Madigan, Miriam Kingston, Davie Phillips, Lelia Doolan and Peter Sheridan. Without their support, encouragement and practical suggestions this book could not have come about. I would also like to thank Seán O Boyle of Columba Press for his patience and guidance throughout.

Contents

The Contributors

Fr Harry Bohan, Chairman of The Céifin Centre, qualified as a sociologist in the University of Wales, and is currently Director of Pastoral Planning in the Diocese of Killaloe and parish priest in Sixmilebridge, Co Clare. In 1973, he founded the Rural Housing Organisation based on the concepts of family and community, to revitalise rural villages and small towns. Through its activities, 2,500 houses were built in 120 communities in thirteen counties.

In 1998, he founded The Céifin Centre for Values-led Change to reflect, debate and direct values-led change in Irish society. He has written extensively on Christianity, spirituality, economic development and on understanding change. Fr Bohan is recognised as one of the leading social commentators in Ireland today. He has broadcast widely on national radio and television, and is also well known for his involvement in sport – Clare hurling in particular.

Sara Burke is a health policy analyst, journalist, writer and broadcaster. Her book, *Irish Apartheid: Healthcare Inequality in Ireland*, was published in June 2009. Sara has a weekly health slot on RTÉ Radio 1's *Drivetime* programme and regularly publishes articles in the national print media. She is in year two of a PhD in health policy. Between 2004 and 2006, she was managing editor in *Village* magazine. She worked in public health policy full time between 1997 and 2004, including two years in the Department of Health. From 1992 to 1997, she worked for Focus Ireland as an outreach worker with homeless teenagers in Dublin.

Professor Tom Collins is Vice President for External Affairs and Dean of Teaching and Learning in NUI Maynooth. Prior to this he was Head of the Education Department, NUI Maynooth and is the former Director of Dundalk Institute of Technology. He was government advisor on both the Green Paper (1998) and White Paper (2000) on Adult Education at which time he was Director of the Centre for Adult and Community Education at NUI Maynooth. He is currently chair of the National Council for Curriculum and Assessment.

Rose Dolan is the course leader of the Post-Graduate Diploma in Education in NUI Maynooth. She is a former second level teacher, a founder of Gluais, the youth leadership development programme for second level pupils and a former adult and community development officer.

Richard Douthwaite is an economist and writer with a special interest in climate and energy issues and in local economic development. His best-known book, *The Growth Illusion: How Economic Growth Enriched the Few, Impoverished the Many and Endangered the Planet* explores the effects that the pursuit of growth has had on the environment and society. His other major book, *Short Circuit* (1996) gives examples of currency, banking, energy and food production systems which communities can use to make themselves less dependent on an increasingly unstable world economy. In *The Ecology of Money* (1999), he calls for changes in the way money is put into circulation so that a stable, sustainable economy can be achieved.

He is a co-founder of Feasta, the Foundation for the Economics of Sustainability, the Dublin-based international network of people who believe that the world's sustainability problems are due to the use of dysfunctional systems and are trying to develop better ones. His current projects include the design and introduction of novel financing arrangements for community energy projects and the management of the Carbon Cycles and Sinks Network which explores ways in which land-based greenhouse gas emissions can be reduced. He lives in Westport, Co Mayo.

JOHN FEEHAN has been described by Kevin Myers as 'one of life's great communicators'. He has researched and written extensively on many facets of Ireland's environmental heritage and history, co-authoring the definitive textbook on Ireland's peatlands, as well as books on the environmental heritage and history of Slieve Bloom and of County Laois. He is the author of *Farming in Ireland: History, Heritage and Environment*, which has been widely acclaimed, while his *Wildflowers of Offaly* was described by Michael Viney as 'a landmark in books about our countryside'. His most recent book is *The Singing Heart of the World: Creation, Evolution and Faith* (Columba Press, 2010).

John is a senior lecturer in the School of Agriculture and Food Science at UCD. He is well known for his television work on the natural and cultural heritage of the Irish landscape, for which he received a Jacobs Television Award. He is also a recipient of the annual Environmental Merit Award of the Chartered Institution of Water and Environmental Management, and of a special award from Bord na Móna for his work in communicating environmental values.

EAMONN HENRY was a founder member of Offaly Sports Partnership in 2003 and has been Sports Partnership Coordinator since 2006. He played Gaelic football for his local club and represented Offaly in athletics in a number of BLOE, Schools and Community Games National finals, as well as becoming area secretary and county delegate for the Community Games at seventeen. A graduate of the Kimmage Manor Development Studies Centre, Eamonn worked overseas for several years on rural development and co-operative marketing projects, and since returning to Ireland has worked in the local development sector. Eamonn cites the establishment of the FAST Kids project with James Nolan as one of the most fulfilling aspects of his work to date.

LIAM HERRICK has been the Executive Director of the Irish Penal Reform Trust (IPRT) since November 2007. IPRT is Ireland's leading non-governmental organisation campaigning for progressive reform of the Irish penal system, based on respect for human rights and the principle that imprisonment should be used only as a sanction of last resort. Before taking up that position, Liam was the first Senior Legislation and Policy Review Officer with the Irish Human Rights Commission, a position he held for four years. He has a broad range of experience in the NGO and State sector, having worked with the Irish Council for Civil Liberties, the Department of Foreign Affairs and the Law Reform Commission. Liam has taught in the School of Social Work and Social Policy at Trinity College Dublin and in the School of Politics and International Relations, University College Dublin, and is currently also a Board member of the Children's Rights Alliance. He lives in Dublin and is married with two children.

HENDRIK W VAN DER KAMP is a practising town planner and Head of the School of Spatial Planning in Dublin Institute of Technology. As well as providing planning advice to community groups, architects, consultants and private developers, he has given advice and acted as an expert evaluator to a range of public sector bodies including government departments and the European Commission. He was a member of the Expert Advisory Group for the National Spatial Strategy and recently chaired a focus group on Sustainability as part of the preparation of the government policy on architecture. He is a Past-President of the Irish Planning Institute and he chaired the Urban Forum between 2006-2008.

SR STANISLAUS KENNEDY is a Religious Sister of Charity and one of Ireland's best-known social innovators. Originally from Co Kerry, she helped establish Kilkenny Social Services in the 1960s. In the 1970s, she was a founder member of the National Federation of Youth Clubs and CARE and co-founded the School of Education in Kilkenny. In the 1980s she founded and remains a Life President of Focus Ireland. In the 1990s Sr Stan founded and is a Director on the Board of the Sanctuary, Dublin. In 2001, she founded Social Innovations Ireland from which the Immigrant Council of Ireland and Young Social Innovators emerged. She is on the Board of the Community Foundation for Ireland. She is also a writer and some of her books include: *Now is the time; A Bundle of Blessings; Gardening the Soul; Seasons of the Day* and most recently *Stillness through my prayers* and an expanded edition of *Now is the time*.

JAMES NOLAN has competed for Ireland at two Olympic Games (Sydney 2000 and Athens 2004), holds a European Indoor silver medal for 1,500m and a European U-23 silver medal for 800m. His national junior (U-20) record for the 800m set in 1996 still stands. James has completed a BSc in Sports Management at UCD, is currently head of Paralympic Athletics with the Paralympic Council of Ireland, middle distance coach at UCD and founder/director of the FAST Kids project.

PAUL O'HARA is leading the development of Ashoka – World Leaders in Social Innovation, in Ireland and Scandinavia, launching key programmes in support of social entrepreneurs. Born in 1978 and raised in the West of Ireland, Paul studied Commerce at NUI, Galway, and Marketing at the Smurfit School of Business, University College Dublin. He spent the next five years working at Unilever Bestfoods and Cadbury Schweppes. An entrepreneur since his teenage years, in 2005 Paul founded a social business called The Hope Concept, and most recently has created the Ashoka Localizer, designed to accelerate the spread of social innovations.

DIARMUID Ó MURCHÚ, a member of the Sacred Heart Missionary Order, and a graduate of Trinity College, Dublin, is a social psychologist most of whose working life has been in social ministry, predominantly in London. In that capacity he has worked as a couple's counsellor, in bereavement work, AIDS-HIV counselling, and latterly with homeless people and refugees. As a workshop leader and group facilitator he has worked in Europe, USA, Canada, Australia, The Philippines, Thailand, India, Peru and in several African countries, facilitating programmes on Adult Faith Development. His best known books include *Quantum Theology* (1996, revised in 2004), *Reclaiming Spirituality* (1998), *Evolutionary Faith* (2002), *Ancestral Grace* (2008), and *Adult Faith: Growing in Wisdom and Understanding* (2010).

EMILY O'REILLY, Ombudsman and Information Commissioner, was appointed to a second six-year term as Ombudsman and Information Commissioner by the President, Mrs Mary McAleese, at a ceremony in Áras an Uachtaráin, on 11 June 2009.

As Ombudsman, Ms O'Reilly is also an ex-officio member of the Standards in Public Office Commission, the Referendum Commission, the Constituency Commission and the Commission for Public Service Appointments. In May 2007, following the introduction of the Access to Information on the Environment Regulations which transposed Directive 2003/4/EC into Irish law, Ms O'Reilly was assigned the additional role of Commissioner for Environmental Information.

Prior to her initial appointment as Ombudsman and Information Commissioner in June 2003, Ms O'Reilly was an accomplished journalist and author whose roles included many years as a political correspondent with prominent print and broadcasting media. She is a native of Tullamore, Co Offaly and is married with five children. Ms O'Reilly is a graduate of University College Dublin and Trinity College Dublin. She was also the recipient of a Niemann Fellowship in Journalism at Harvard University. In December 2008 Ms O'Reilly was awarded a Doctor of Laws by the National University of Ireland in recognition of her contribution to public service and to human rights.

EMER Ó SIOCHRÚ is qualified as an Architect and Development and Planning Surveyor and is Director of EOS Future Design which designs and develops sustainable systems and settlements. She is also Director of Smart Taxes, a policy development network which researches and promotes land / site value taxes and environmental levies and tariffs for local bio-energy generation.

She is a member of the Sustainability Task Force of the Royal Institute of Architects of Ireland, Building Regulations Advisory Board, National Rural Network and a representative on the Environmental Pillar of Social Partnership.

Emer Ó Siochrú co-founded Feasta; the Foundation for the Economics of Sustainability in 1998. In 2004 she led the ENLIVEN project in Feasta with Irish Rural Link that researched the potential of renewable energy in rural villages. She has served on Comhar, the National Sustainable Development Partnership and on Irish Environmental Network when she co-edited the IEN submission on the National Sustainable Development Strategy.

MARY LEE RHODES is the Director of the MSc in International Management at Trinity College, Dublin. She has an MBA from Wharton and completed her PhD in Public Management at Trinity College. She also has an MSc from the London School of Economics in Systems Analysis & Design and a BA in Economics from Yale University. Dr Rhodes has a broad range of experience in business and public management including thirteen years in banking operations and technology with JP Morgan, and two years as an economic analyst with the US Department of Agriculture. She is a current or former member of the Board of Directors for several non-profit organisations including Simon Communities of Ireland, Cluid Housing and Taney Village Ltd, and served on the Audit Committee of the Office of the Comptroller and Auditor General. Her research is in public management and complex systems and she is currently working on a book on this topic to be published by Routledge in 2010.

MICHAEL STARRETT, a native of Co Tyrone, was appointed as the Heritage Council's first Chief Executive in August 1996. A graduate ecologist and biologist with post graduate qualifications in education and landscape management he has almost 30 years experience in the areas of heritage management and policy development. His professional qualifications include membership of the Landscape Institute ALI (UK) and the Irish Landscape Institute as well as the Institute of Sport, Parks and Leisure (MISPAL). In addition to a career path that has seen him work in Northern Ireland, Scotland and the Republic of Ireland he has extensive European experience through his membership of the Federation of National and Nature Parks of Europe, a pan European body with 400 members in 38 different countries. He was the first Irishman to be elected as President of the Federation from 2002-2005. He is also a member of the IUCN's World Commission on Protected Areas. Michael has travelled extensively studying legislation and systems that allow the sustainable management and development of cultural and natural landscapes. He recently completed a Masters in Management Practice at Trinity College Dublin. Michael lives in Kilkenny with his wife Giliane and their three children.

PATRICK SUTTON graduated from Dartington College of Arts with a BA (Hons) Theatre. He has recently received his MA in screenwriting from IADT. He is director of The Gaiety School of Acting, The National Theatre School of Ireland and Smock Alley Theatre. He is a former artistic director of TEAM Theatre Company and The Wexford Arts Centre. He is a former board member of The Arts Council, Culture Ireland, Project Arts Centre, Storytellers Theatre Company and The Irish Museum of Modern Art. He is currently a board member of Smock Alley Theatre, The Gaiety School of Acting, the Arts for Peace Foundation and the Lisa Richards Agency. He has recently been appointed to the governing authority of DIT. As a writer he has written Iscariot, Magdalen and The Butte (Montana) Trilogy.

Introduction

The idea for this book came to me from listening to a number of media interviewees claiming that it would be 'some considerable time before we were back to where we were.'

This made me feel uneasy on several counts. Should we really be seeking to get back on the boom treadmill as quickly as possible? Had the boom really been so great for the vast majority of Irish citizens? How far had it benefited our schools and hospitals, or improved our rural and urban landscapes? Did people paying huge mortgages for over-priced houses, or commuting long distances to work, really believe that this was 'as good as it gets'? Along with a lot of anger and blame, the sentiment of getting back to where we were seemed to be the predominant one in the media in 2009.

However, there is now a collective recognition that the crisis provides an opportunity for constructive change. Initiatives such as Martin McAleese's *Your Country, Your Call* competition, and the *Renewing the Republic* series of articles in the *Irish Times* are evidence of this. We have been given an opportunity to question and re-think our values and those of our society. Can we instigate a change in attitudes and culture towards taking action primarily for the longer-term common good rather than for immediate individual gain? And can we make the leap of understanding to realise that everyone benefits from a more equal society?

In reality, getting back to where we were is neither a desirable nor, in the longer-term, a viable option, as many of the contributors to this book ably demonstrate. The speed with which so many of our pillars of apparent certainty have collapsed in the last two years demonstrates that radical change in every aspect of our lives and society needs to become a matter of priority, not just for policy-makers and those who govern us, but for everyone.

As an immediately practical example, our lifestyles today are completely based on the assumption that we can and will continue to consume the same level of fossil fuels indefinitely. Yet this cannot be the case, and our future depends on the willingness and energy we can now muster to embrace that inevitable change. We can resist it, or we can harness our resourcefulness and face an uncertain future with at least a pioneering sense of creativity and adventure.

If we are serious about questioning our current economic model and the direction and shape of Irish society in the future, the contributors to this book offer us some of the tools we will need to make this transition less painful.

The solutions and scenarios put forward in the following pages are evidence of a new way of thinking – one that is kinder and more empathetic, both to the environment and to individual citizens, one that is collaborative and co-operative rather than competitive, and one that is resilient and adaptable to external changes, rather than rigid and inflexible.

I am extremely grateful to all the contributors who have supported this project for their generosity in devoting their time and thought towards the possibilities for Ireland's future. In particular I would like to thank Dr John Feehan for his encouragement and suggestions from the very outset.

Finally, two highly valuable initiatives will benefit from the sales of this book – Feasta and the Céifin Centre for Values-Led Change. Feasta, the Foundation for the Economics of Sustainability, aims to identify the characteristics of a truly sustainable society, articulate how the necessary transition can be effected, and promote the implementation of the measures required for this purpose. The Céifin Centre aims to generate the capacity for debate on issues of social change.

Further information on both can be found at www.feasta.org and www.ceifin.com.

Susannah Kingston
August 2010

CHAPTER ONE

Economy
A Choice of Two Futures: A Vision for 2050

Richard Douthwaite

2050 is a significant year. If the world is to have a reasonable chance of avoiding a disastrous, rapid and uncontrollable shift to a much warmer climate, it is the date by which the burning of coal, gas and oil – as opposed to their use as raw materials – has to end. Organising the world's affairs so that perhaps 9 billion people can live reasonably well without these energy sources will be quite some achievement. A lot of sharing will be involved and the consumption gap between the rich and powerful and the average person will have to narrow quite a lot. In other words, we need a scenario which brings about an Enlightened Transition.

The likelihood is, however, that those making decisions on behalf of humanity will lack enlightenment. The rich and powerful – a group that, in global terms, certainly includes us – will insist on maintaining their position and, although they will not expect it, their refusal to budge will bring the world economy crashing down, sweeping away their wealth and their power. Many of them, along with billions of others, will lose their lives. All that is likely to remain are small, self-sufficient settlements around the world whose inhabitants scrape by at a very low level. I'll call this scenario Enforced Localisation. In this chapter, I want to give some idea of how each of these scenarios might play out and what the economy – and, as a result, everyday life – would be like in 2050 if it did.

Most people imagine that life in 2050 will be quite like life today but with added high technology. Unfortunately, however, there isn't even a slight possibility of such a life at all as there simply won't be enough energy to deliver it. True, there's a still a lot of fossil fuel left underground. The problem is that it takes energy to get it out and the amount of energy and sophisticated equipment required for its extraction is increasing. This is because energy companies naturally exploit the easiest resources first – the thickest coal seams and the shallowest onshore deposits of gas and oil. It is only after the best resources have been used up that they move on to the trickier ones – the thinner coal seams plagued with geological faults, or the oil and gas fields under the Arctic ice or in deep water offshore.

These more difficult resources require much more capital investment and have higher running costs. In other words, more energy has to be invested and spent to release the energy they contain. So, while it took the energy in one barrel of oil to produce a hundred times that amount of energy in Texas in the 1930s, that same energy investment produces only 15 barrels of oil today. It's the same with iron and other types of ore too – poorer deposits are having to be mined and it takes more energy to separate the good parts from waste.

As a result, as the years pass, increasing amounts of energy are going to be required to produce the world's energy and mineral requirements if the same number of people is going to be able to live in the way we do today. Increase the number of people from 6.5 billion to the 9 billion expected in 2050, and even more energy has to be applied. In short, more energy is going to be needed in future than is used today.

But it will be impossible to supply this increased amount of energy. Indeed, I think that it is highly unlikely that we will even be able to maintain the current net energy supply – that is, the energy we actually get to use after the energy cost of extracting and delivering that energy is taken away. When an energy resource gives, say, ten times more energy back than it took to extract it, 90% of the energy it contains is available for human use. However, when the figure drops to 5 to 1, only 80% is available, and after that, a rapidly rising proportion of the energy in the resource has to be used to produce it. At 3 to 1, for example, only two-thirds is available.

Now you might think that it would be worth producing oil for energy use so long as you got back slightly more energy from the oil than it took you to extract it. However, that would mean that the economy devoted almost all its efforts to getting its oil and had almost no energy left for doing anything else.

Professor Charles Hall of New York State University, who developed the energy-return-on-energy-invested (EROEI) idea after investigating why fish bothered to use energy to migrate, believes that, in view of the amount of energy it takes to run our civilisation, its energy sources have to have an average return significantly higher than 3:1 for it to persist.

Chris Vernon, who co-edits the Oil Drum website, is another EROEI expert. He says that although there might be enough oil for global extraction to run at approximately half today's level in 2050, the amount of usable energy humanity will get from it depends on the rate at which the EROEI declines. 'If the EROEI declines faster than it did in the US during the 20th century, it is possible that the average EROEI will be so low that, by mid-century, oil will cease to be a significant net energy source,' he says. Exactly the same argument applies to the net amount of energy available from coal and gas.

2050 will therefore be an energy-constrained time whichever scenario is followed. If we try to think ourselves through both scenarios, the major differences that emerge between them are due to the net energy available per head and the number of people each is trying to support. During an enforced localisation, many deaths would be inevitable as production and supply systems break down, whereas an enlightened transition would have the resources to support a larger number.

Low-energy societies have low levels of output per person and consequently require most people to be involved in producing their basic needs. The net energy *per capita* figure will therefore determine each economy's sophistication. Neither scenario will deliver a society able to afford the numbers of full-time writers, artists, musicians, broadcasters, scientists, teachers, office staff, healthcare professionals, teachers and social workers we have today, nor will so wide a range of goods and services be available. An early symptom of this will be 'peak student' when the proportion of young people in further education begins to fall. However, while an enlightened transition might produce a society that operates at a 1950s level, an enforced localisation might mean a return to the Middle Ages. Here's how someone writing in 2050 might explain how their economy had developed under each scenario.

Enlightened Transition
Extract from *Modern Irish History for Schools*, Fallons, Dublin, 2050, Chapter 2, 'The Rise and Fall of the Consumer Economy'

Towards the end of 2011, the G-20, the world's twenty most powerful governments at the time, realised rather belatedly that the sharp rise in energy costs between 2004 and 2008 was the fundamental reason for the debt problems which had caused the near-collapse of the global banking system in 2008. The high cost of energy was, in turn, due to the increasing difficulty of keeping up with the world's growing demand for oil. Production after 2004 had stayed almost level despite a quadrupling of the price. The increased price meant that so much money had to be spent by consumers, on buying oil or commodities made using it, that they did not have enough money for other things, including, in some cases, paying interest on their debts.

Indeed, a lot of the extra money the consumers spent on buying oil and other commodities had contributed to the debt crisis. It had been deposited by the producers in banks in the consumer countries. When this money was loaned out, it was the final straw which made the rich-countries' already-large debt burden unsupportable. To prevent this happening again, the governments introduced a system to share out what economists call the 'scarcity rent' – the excess profits which the energy producers had been able to make because of the growing shortage. They set up what was, in effect, a buyers' ring just like the ones which dishonest antique dealers initiate before an auction. In a ring, the dealers decide which of them is to bid for an item and the maximum he or she is to pay. Then, afterwards, they hold a private auction among themselves to determine who actually gets the antique they all want. They do this to ensure that the extra money which would have gone to the vendor if they had bid against each other in the original auction stays within the group and does not leak away unnecessarily to a member of the public.

The point of the G-20 energy-buying ring was exactly the same – to prevent excess money going to fossil fuel producers in times of scarcity and plunging the world into an economic depression. Instead, a large part of the difference between the rolling five-year price the ring negotiated with the oil producers – the arrangement was extended later to include coal and natural gas – and the price it got in the monthly auctions which shared out the fuel amongst the ring's members was invested in developing sources of renewable energy.

In effect, the system imposed a variable-rate, worldwide tax on fossil fuel use, although strictly it was not a tax but a quota. This would have been quite impossible to achieve during those years had it been proposed in the UN. The 'tax rate' went up when the economy boomed and fell back if it slowed, providing an economic stabilisation mechanism. And the 'tax' was truly global. The G-20 negotiators knew that, despite the fact that its members bought about 80% of the world's oil, they had to get as many smaller countries into the ring as possible so that the minnows did not deal with the producers directly and offer them a better price.

Some of the minnows bargained hard over the share of the 'tax' revenue they would get before giving their support. Indeed, within the G-20 itself, there was a lot of tough negotiation between India and China on the one hand who wanted the share-out to be solely on the basis of each country's population, and the US and the EU on the other, who wanted shares to be on the basis of current levels of energy use. The latter pointed out that, because their economies were so heavily dependent on fossil fuels, they needed to invest large sums to phase them out. In the end, though, a compromise was worked out. About 10% of the money went to governments to distribute to overcome the increase in fuel-poverty the scheme inevitably brought about. A similar amount was used to pay a Carbon Maintenance Fee to reward countries which maintained and increased the amount of carbon in their biomass and soils. The remainder was placed in a revolving loan fund to finance projects to reduce fossil energy requirements against the day they ran out.

'The governments realised that fossil energy was running out rapidly and that they needed to ensure that a very high proportion of the money collected by the energy buyers' ring was invested in the transition to renewable energy' wrote Richard Douthwaite, the economist who proposed the ring solution in 2021. 'The ring did that. It gave non-fossil energy projects a guarantee of the high prices they required to attract investors and it also provided a lot of the finance the projects required.'

The loan fund pioneered the energy bond system we use today. Instead of setting a fixed rate of interest, the conventional method of allocating money at the time, the fund bought bonds from energy project promoters. These bonds entitled the fund to the revenue from the sale of a specific share of the project's output in a specific year rather than a specific cash payment. If, for example, a large project offered bonds for gigawatt-hours (one million kilowatt-hours) in five years' time, the fund would base the price it offered for each GWh on its estimate of how much that power might be worth when it came to be sold. This system suited both power project promoters and investors. It took a lot of the market risk off the promoters' shoulders. All they had to worry about was producing the power. The price that they got for it was secondary. From the fund's and other investors' point of view, however, the system meant that they put their money where the power produced was expected to be of most value. This arrangement sidestepped the argument of whether rich countries or poorer ones should get the lion's share of the fund's investments and pleased economists who thought it 'efficient'.

In Ireland, the ESB set up a new division, ESB Community Energy, to take advantage of the fund's money. Communities would invite ESBCE to survey their local renewable energy resources and prepare a costed development plan. Then, if enough people were prepared to commit themselves to buying the power for the required number of years at the price the plan found necessary, ESBCE would let the construction contracts and manage the project on behalf of the community energy company until all the bonds had matured. At that point, the community company, which was then owned by its customers in proportion to the amount of power they had bought, owned all the assets outright. It could manage the project itself or contract with a specialist company to do so.

'The big advantage of agreeing to buy energy from an ESBCE project was that, although the power might have cost a few cents more per unit than that from the ESB itself, most of the money you paid was actually a form of saving because it went to pay off the bonds' Douthwaite wrote. 'Once that debt is cleared, the community company can sell the power at the actual cost of production and delivery – about a third of the previous price. However, most of the community energy companies do not bring the price down until a customer retires. At that point, the companies also begin buying the retired person's investment from him or her and selling it on to the next generation. As a result of getting cheap power and their money back, some older people are getting almost free power.'

Although there was a lot of opposition to the oil-buyers' ring when it was introduced in 2012, once it was in place attitudes changed because of the employment and economic stability it brought. Even the energy producers came to like it because, rather than relying on an unstable market to determine how much they earned, they could negotiate a price for their fuel based on the increasing cost of production. And, when the ring began to reduce its annual orders for climate change reasons, they liked it even more because they were able to conserve their stock in the ground and sell it more slowly at higher and higher real prices. They got a much better return from holding on to their energy resource than holding shares on Wall Street.

'The real value of oil and gas is as a raw material for petrochemicals, not to be burned,' Douthwaite reports Prince Saud al-Faisal, the Saudi oil minister, as saying in 2019. 'I'm not worried about stopping selling oil for fuel by 2050. I'd like to stop it sooner. If we hang on to our resources now we can sell them to make plastics for hundreds of years.'

The realisation that fossil energy was running out and that less energy was likely to be available in future brought many other changes. Perhaps the most far-reaching was the ending of the extraordinary practice of allowing commercial banks to create money out of nothing and then charge their customers – including governments – interest for it when they lent it into circulation. This massive subsidy to the financial sector was one of the reasons that, at the time of the 2008 debt crisis, it commandeered over 30% of the incomes generated by what were then the wealthiest economies in the world.

Many governments' initially attributed the crisis to the bankers' personal greed and sought to prevent a repeat by limiting their bonuses so that they had less incentive to lend irresponsibly.

However, when the EU and the US found that their economies were in such bad shape that none of their banks' customers was willing or able to go any further into debt and that, as a result, their national money supplies were contracting as more past loans were repaid than new ones taken out, they had no choice but to take money creation under national control to avoid a catastrophic depression. In a co-ordinated move designed to prevent speculators playing one currency off against another, the European Central Bank, the Federal Reserve and the Bank of England held a joint press conference to announce that they were all going to use quantitative easing to create money which they would give, rather than lend, to their governments to spend into circulation. The 'gifts' would ensure that national debts did not rise any further and the drastic public spending cuts, which had been causing massive street protests, could end. Henceforward, they said, the commercial banks were to cease money creation. Their activities would be confined to operating the money transfer system and lending out their depositors' savings.

The European Commission was alarmed by the prospect that for at least the next decade, the ECB would be giving member states large amounts of money to spend in ways over which it, the Commission, had no control. This threatened to alter the balance of power in the EU by making national governments less beholden to the centre. To avoid this, the Commission arranged that most of the ECB money had to be passed on to regional governments rather than the national ones. This changed Ireland from being one of the most centrally-governed countries in Europe to one in which its four regional governments had real power, a power which they copperfastened when they all launched regional currencies to supplement the Euros they were receiving. These currencies gave the regions the economic flexibility they required to handle the massive changes going on by allowing them to change their exchange rates in relation to the others.

Other effects were equally profound. As a result of the ECB money, the debt-burden carried by the Eurozone economies quickly shrank, along with the size of their banking systems. Up to that point, the banks had decided what sort of projects went ahead by selecting those to which they gave loans. Only those which promised attractive profits and whose promoters could offer adequate security were approved. This had been extraordinarily distorting because it meant that projects which promised to produce benefits for large numbers of people but whose value could not be captured by selling them to the beneficiaries had not been able to borrow and could only go ahead if the state had given them a grant. As a result of this distortion, the commercial, for-profit part of the economy grew massively in relation to the non-monetised and non-commercial parts. After the change in the way money was issued, though, since the state was being given money rather than having to borrow it, it was initially able to make more capital and current funding available to non-commercial projects, many of which were community based. Different support channels were established so that a wide range of projects went ahead. In essence, investments no longer had to produce a monetary return. Other types of return became acceptable.

These balmy days did not last long and the amount of investment that the state could fund fell rapidly. One reason for this was that, once all the debt-based money had been repaid or written-off, no new non-debt money had to be spent into use by the government to replace it. This gave it less to spend, particularly as the money economy was shrinking anyway and less currency was needed to provide adequate liquidity. However, the state continued to inject some new money into the economy each year because it claimed that having a mild inflation enabled businesses in the overgrown parts of the economy, such as the motor trade and retailing, to decline gradually and that this was less disruptive for their employees and the wider economy than having individual firms collapse overnight.

The second reason for the lack of investment was that the cost of energy and raw materials rose massively and that the very limited amount of capital funding that the state had available did not go very far. Indeed, very few new buildings, public or private, have gone up since 2025. It has been far better to use the county's limited resources to repair and adapt existing ones rather than build new but, even so, a lot of the buildings erected in the early part of this century have become derelict or fallen into disrepair. All the bigger urban centres experienced a decline because of the loss of service-sector jobs, and this is especially true in the Dublin region.

Rural areas generally, and the West in particular, have fared much better and a lot of the 150,000 houses that had seemed surplus to requirements when the debt crisis burst the property bubble had occupants by 2020 as a result of the employment created by two other consequences of energy buyers' ring – the development of the ocean energy industry and the spread of biorefineries. Indeed, the distribution of population today is densest along the west coast, just as it was immediately before the Great Famine of the 1840s.

The early biorefineries were very crude. They simply crushed leafy plants such as miscanthus, Japanese knotweed, buddleia and hemp in water to extract the protein which was then fed to chickens and pigs to replace soya from Brazil. The remaining pulp was pyrolysed by being heated in a closed container to produce synthetic natural gas and later a liquid fuel for diesel engines. Gradually, however, more stages were added to the process and a much wider range of chemicals was produced to replace those which had been sourced from oil.

The offshore energy industry has also created thousands of skilled and relatively well-paid jobs in formerly remote areas like that around Belmullet in Co Mayo, where the influx of activity stemmed from the establishment of the Wave Energy Test Station there in 2010. Ports like Killybegs, Rossaveal, Galway, Foynes and Castletownbere also became hubs for energy-related developments such as the submarine cable factory at Foynes and the floating marine turbine assembly plant in an old shipyard at New Ross.

Despite a slow start, it is fair to say that Ireland went through its energy transition more easily than most countries, largely because it had the second-best offshore resource (after Scotland) and more under-utilised agricultural land per head of population than anywhere else in Western Europe. From importing almost all its energy, it is now a net exporter. However, it seems unlikely that this profound change would have come about had the energy-buying ring not been established and the market for fossil energy tightly controlled.

Enforced Localisation

Extracts from handwritten entries in a notebook found on Gabriel Dillon's desk after his death in 2051. The notes were headed 'For my grandchildren'.

I was surprised how quickly the global economy fell apart after what we called the 'credit crunch' in 2008 and 2009. The first warning of how bad things might get came after an American bank called Lehman Brothers, that went in for a lot of speculation, collapsed in 2008. Lehman's owed a lot of money to other banks and world trade almost stopped for a few days because exporters were worried that these other banks might fail too and, if they accepted payment for their goods through these other banks, their money might be lost. So, until they were sure their payments were safe, they refused to deliver and the supply of oil to Europe nearly broke down. Row upon row of oil tankers had to lie at anchor off Kharg Island in Saudi Arabia for several days waiting until the situation was resolved and they could be filled. If the problem had gone on for much longer, the world's transport system would have started breaking down then rather than later on.

But no one paid much attention at the time. I can remember reading about the tankers in an article written by a friend of mine in Dublin called David Korowicz, a brilliant physicist who got interested in the risks that the western economic system was running after seeing how it was making life more risky and less sustainable for villages in Kyrgyzstan where he had lived for some years. He told me once that a friend of his had found that 49 different types of apple tree were grown in the village in which she was living. The sweet ones were sold in the city, the villagers ate some of the rest themselves and fed the remainder to their animals. Then USAID advisers came along and proposed that the villagers should fell all the apple trees whose fruit could not be sold and grow saleable ones instead. They would make more money that way. And if they used artificial fertiliser they could grow more vegetables and, if they sold those too, they would be able to pay for their children to go to university and get well-paid jobs in what they called 'the knowledge economy'. The trouble with all this was that some years, the saleable varieties produced no apples at all whereas, with their mixture of trees, the villagers could be sure that some of them would crop even in bad years. And if many villages used fertiliser on their vegetables so they could sell them, the price of vegetables would come down and they'd be worse off after paying for the fertiliser and the loan that financed it. And there were no jobs for graduates in the city in any case.

David told me that the whole proposal had showed him how economic processes could trap people so that they could only continue losing autonomy and resilience – or go bust, and he had returned to Dublin to try to fight the mindset that had dreamt such a system up.

Anyway, David's article explained that we could only afford all the things that we enjoyed at that time – the cars, the computers, the televisions, the foreign holidays – because of two things – the fossil energy which subsidised their production and the economies that came from producing them on a huge scale for a global market. He said that, just as there had been a positive feed-back on the way up, with bigger markets enabling prices to be cut and so creating even bigger markets still, there would be a similar positive feedback but in reverse on the way down. Higher energy prices would reduce demand, which would then put production costs up, which would mean that demand fell even further. This would drive some firms out of business, so that spares for their equipment would become either unobtainable or very costly if they had to be made specially. Manufacturing and delivery systems would become increasingly unreliable, and things would break down very quickly once the chips in telephones and computers began to fail or the power generation people could not get key components.

He was right about this too, but I'm getting ahead of myself. The first thing to cause a massive disruption was the complete breakdown of the global banking system after Greece defaulted on its debts. It turned out that German and French banks had been enabling the Greek economy to import far more than it exported for many years and that, as the huge sums they were owed were unlikely to be repaid, they were bankrupt too, so bankrupt in fact that neither government had sufficient resources to rescue them. Of course, they owed money to other banks. These had to close too as no one would risk putting money in them anymore. The upshot was that large numbers of people in the richer countries lost all their savings and although notes and coins denominated in a currency called the Euro continued to be used in Ireland for a few months, no one outside the European Union would touch them. It was a re-run of the post-Lehman Brothers situation but magnified a million times.

Eventually, barter systems were set up to fill the gap left by the collapse of an important international currency. For example, chains of big shops – we called them supermarkets – would buy Irish meat and milk products and ship them to England to sell and then use the English money they collected to buy British goods for their Irish stores. These dealers spent their English money as quickly as they could because, although Britain actually avoided defaulting on its debts by the skin of its teeth, no one wanted to hold its money for a minute longer than necessary in case it did.

This sort of trading was all right for simple goods but it was much harder to get hold of the more unusual products needed to keep key facilities like radio transmitters operating. Actually, some Russians helped the government's radio station – it was called RTÉ – with this in 2013, but I don't know why it closed later. The Russians were using experience they had gained when their currency, the rouble, collapsed in the 1990s. I can remember reading a story in *The New York Times* at the time about the way that Splav, a company in Novgorod which made valves for the oil, gas, chemical and nuclear industries, had managed to keep its 4,000-strong workforce busy with only 10% of its invoices being paid in cash. The company even set up a chain of chemist's shops to sell the drugs it received in payment from some customers. It paid its local taxes in Volga cars, road tax with excavators and medical insurance with ambulances.

A staff of fifty developed its deals. One particularly complex one to finance a sale to the Balakovo nuclear power station involved the power company cancelling the overdue electricity bill of a foundry in Kazakhstan on the basis that the latter would send castings to a factory in the Russian republic of Bashkiriya, which then sent its product to the Lipetsk Metallurgical Combine, which then provided sheet metal for a half dozen car and truck factories in Russia and Belarus. The vehicle manufacturers then sent cars and trucks to Splav, some of which it sold for cash. Others were used to pay some of its taxes. Splav had to mark up its prices to make the barter sales work because a lot of the goods it received had to be sold or exchanged at a discount.

This was exactly what people had to do for several months after the collapse of the Euro until replacement national currencies were launched and currency dealers had set themselves up to operate independently of the collapsed banks, which were all being wound up.

This was the time my wages stopped. The government simply didn't have the means to pay people like me as it could not borrow and no taxes were being paid. I carried on working at the hospital for as long as I could – at least we got free meals while we were on duty – but as the situation dragged on and muggings became a severe problem, Granny and I decided we had to move to the holiday cottage we had in Clare where there was at least some land on which we could establish a garden.

It was just as well that we moved when we did because that was the year that bird 'flu returned but in a much more virulent form than it had been a few years earlier. Or perhaps it was that people's resistance was lower because they were much less well fed. Life expectancy had already fallen, just as it did in Russia when the Soviet Union broke down. I once read a book about the Black Death which suggested that it killed as many as it did because the population at the time had grown beyond the limits of each country's food resources. But it wasn't just that people were in a weaker state. Another reason for the appalling death toll was that the government could not have afforded to import a vaccine even if one had been available. (I heard that one was, but it was officially denied at the time.) I don't think many of my colleagues at the hospital survived.

About half the world's population probably died either from the 'flu or the disruption that followed it. No one knows for sure since there's no way to count. Since then, everyone has been trying to live as best they can from the resources of their area, including the debris the consumer boom left behind. As you know, I've managed quite well. We always had the woodstove and the roofs and floors of derelict houses burn pretty well.

Since the ESB went off for the last time, I've been able to fix an old truck alternator to a set of paddles in the stream below the house and we can have electric light for as long as I can continue to find the bulbs. There used to be lots in abandoned cars but as several people in the area are using them they are getting scarce. I've got a radio, too. I keep checking but it's several years since there was anything on. And some things are better. Since the 'flu, the gangs that used to trek out of Limerick to steal my potatoes and chickens don't come any more. They took Mr McCarthy's horse one time – for meat I imagine – which meant that he could no longer use his plough. We should have protected ourselves against this sort of thing as it's just what happened in Germany when their money was destroyed by inflation after the First World War. The men who robbed us are probably dead, just as I will be soon. What a world I'm handing on.

* * *

These two scenarios are, I hope, equally plausible but not, I fear, equally possible. Enforced Localisation is the default position. It is almost certain to come about if we go on as we are. David Korowicz' article on which my exploration is based is available on the Feasta website, www.feasta.org. The solutions proposed in the Enlightened Transition scenario are developed in an article of mine which is also on the Feasta site. The adoption of that scenario requires a recognition that humanity is at an historic turning point and new solutions are urgently needed to avert a large-scale die-off. It's up to us all to insist that our governments make the right choice and one way to do that is to make it clear that we don't believe them when they claim to see the green shoots of recovery and confidently predict that the boom times will return.

CHAPTER TWO

Governance
In The Public Interest: Lessons from the Ombudsman's Experience

Emily O'Reilly

The text of this chapter is an address by Emily O'Reilly to the Institute of Public Administration & Chartered Institute of Public Finance and Accounting – Conference on Good Governance, on 9 March 2010, and printed here with her permission.

I am pleased to have been invited to address this conference. The theme, 'Good Governance: Values and Culture or Rules and Regulations', is timely. It comes at a point when even the economically illiterate now realise that poor governance in a number of our key private and public institutions lies at the heart of the downturn. The theme also resonates with my work as Ombudsman and Information Commissioner. For the last 26 years the overarching work of the Ombudsman's Office has been about nothing less than the transformation of the culture of the public service, turning it away from the inward gaze and protection of self and forcing it instead to direct that gaze towards the public and their needs. Our work under FOI brings with it a similar intent. We have had great successes and some, though few, disappointments. I do intend however – at a later stage in this address – to use this platform and this theme, to talk about one current and very significant event for my Office, the treatment by the Oireachtas of my investigation into the so-called Lost at Sea scheme. I will track a line that runs from maladministration in a government department right through to poor governance at the very highest level of this State.

I will submit that the economic and political crises that face this country will never be dealt with unless the culture and values of the political and administrative classes undergo profound change. An investigation by an Ombudsman may seem small scale in comparison to the huge financial challenges around us, yet it is a microcosm nonetheless of the faultlines within our system.

Over the last 18 months or so, the word governance has begun to seep into every day discourse much as 'fiscal rectitude' did in the 1970s and the triumvirate of openness, transparency and accountability did in the 1990s. It is the new panacea for our economic and political ills but it is open to question as to how successful the proselytising of the need for good governance will be in the absence of the cultural change I have just mentioned. Observe, after all, what happened to the last publicly approved panacea.

To recap, the need for openness, transparency and accountability was cued by the slew of political/business scandals of the late 20th century. Rules and regulations were heralded in through the Freedom of Information Act but within a very short time it became clear that the old cultures and values still nestled largely undisturbed at the heart of the administration.

The Act was barely five years old when the government rolled back some of its more sensitive provisions and introduced a scale of up-front fees, alien creatures in many international FOI regimes. As I have often said, following these measures, the Act was seriously winded but it wasn't stretchered off the pitch. Very significant and effective use has been made of the Act even since its curtailment and, ironically, never more so than during this current economic downturn. Yet the curtailment of the FOI Act was an example of how legally binding rules and regulations still failed to defeat the prevailing values and culture of secrecy. There is no doubt that 12 years of FOI have brought about some significant change for the better, but as I will point out later, we still have quite a distance to travel.

And so to governance. On the face of it, a rather esoteric topic for students of public administration, yet now clearly recognised, through the prism of this recession, as the bedrock of good management and good government. The spectacular failings in the banks, in FÁS, have given us real-life examples of what is not good governance. Similarly, the awaited reports on the Dublin Docklands Development Authority will, according to media commentators, expose serious failings of corporate governance in that organisation. We have also witnessed serious lapses in governance in the Financial Regulator's office. The Oireachtas itself has not escaped attention either with many commentators and indeed Oireachtas members themselves asking whether it is fit for purpose. Even members of the Cabinet itself, the body which wields ultimate power, publicly lament the ineffectual nature of much of what passes for parliamentary activity. This from a speech by Transport Minister Noel Dempsey:

> We should return Dáil Éireann to a central place in public thinking. It should be the battleground for ideas, the location for intellectual debate, where the brightest and best work in concert to achieve optimal results over the long-term, not cheap point-scoring in the short term.

On the question of how to do good governance there is no shortage of material available – the OECD Report, *Ireland: Towards an Integrated Public Service*, the report of the task force on the public service, *Transforming Public Services*, the Department of Finance publication, *Code of Practice for the Governance of State Bodies* and the Chairpersons' Forum publication, *A Chairperson's Guide to Good Governance*. And in the meantime, endless handwringing about which is the best way forward. Is it more rules and regulations, or should it be driven by values and culture? Or is it some combination of both?

Before dealing with these questions, let me first say a few words about the importance of good governance in managing and directing an Ombudsman's Office. The British and Irish Ombudsman Association (BIOA), of which I am the current Chairperson, recently developed a guide to the principles of good governance for ombudsman offices and other complaint handling bodies. As I said in my introduction to the guide:

> Whatever governance arrangements are in place in any complaint-handling scheme, it is vital that they support and promote the integrity of the scheme and office-holder and, above all, protect the independence of the office-holder, particularly from those over whom the scheme has jurisdiction.

And so, for example, in the case of my own office, the fact that it operates under statute, has its own vote, is staffed by civil servants of the State and not civil servants of the government, reports to the Oireachtas and has an office-holder who is appointed by the President, following a resolution passed by the Oireachtas, all helps to support and promote the integrity and independence of the office.

The guide identified six principles of good governance, namely: independence, openness and transparency, accountability, integrity, clarity of purpose and effectiveness. I don't propose to elaborate here on these principles; I expect it is reasonably clear that they would represent the cornerstones for the governance of any organisation. And finally, just to be clear that we all understand what we mean by governance, the guide includes the following definition:

> The way organisations are directed and controlled to ensure that they are effective in achieving their objectives.

As Ombudsman and Information Commissioner, I do not have a role in policing the governance arrangements of public bodies, but arising from my office's daily interactions with those bodies, we are well placed to form a view on the competing roles of values and culture and rules and regulations in how they go about their business.

As Ombudsman I examine complaints of maladministration against government departments, local authorities, the public health service and An Post. I also have certain complaint functions in relation to the Disability Act, 2005. I make recommendation for redress where appropriate, and I report annually to the Oireachtas on the work of my office. If a public body chooses to reject my recommendations, I may make a special report to the Oireachtas. This has happened only twice in the 26 year history of the office; in 2002 and in 2009. As a result of Oireachtas intervention, and deliberation by the Joint Oireachtas Committee on Finance and the Public Service, the recommendations in the 2002 report, *Redress for Taxpayers*, were accepted by the Revenue Commissioners. However, at the time of writing, and as mentioned earlier, the recommendations in my 2009 report, 'Lost at Sea', remain rejected following a Dáil vote not to refer the report to the Joint Committee on Agriculture, Fisheries and Food for further deliberation. A subsequent attempt at a meeting of the Committee to have the report considered also failed. I will come back to this later.

As Information Commissioner my principal role is to review the decisions of public bodies under the Freedom of Information Acts, 1997 and 2003. I make binding decisions which may be appealed to the High Court but only on a point of law. I report annually to the Oireachtas on the work of my office. My remit as Information Commissioner is wider than that as Ombudsman; there are more than 520 bodies subject to the FOI Acts but some significant bodies remain exempted, including for example, An Garda Síochána, the Vocational Education Committees and of particular significance in current economic circumstances is the continued exclusion of the Central Bank, the Irish Financial Services Regulatory Authority, the National Treasury Management Agency, and, indeed, the newly established National Assets Management Agency.

The principal function of the Act as detailed in the Long Title is

> ... to enable members of the public to obtain access, to the greatest extent possible, consistent with the public interest and the right to privacy, to information in the possession of public bodies ... to provide for a right of access to records held by such bodies, for necessary exceptions to that right ...

Given such an inspiring Long Title, it is difficult to reconcile it with the continued exclusion of the above public bodies. But not only are some public bodies not included but in recent years a practice has developed of removing public bodies or functions of public bodies from the scope of the FOI Acts. Examples of functions that have been removed are the enforcement functions of the Health and Safety Authority, the road safety functions now carried out by the Road Safety Authority, and the functions of the Land Registry and the Registry of Deeds now performed by the Property Registration Authority. I am also aware that a proposal to remove from the scope of FOI, records relating to the enforcement functions of the National Employment Rights Authority is being actively considered. I do not accept these exclusions, or the rationale behind them. In particular, I am concerned that removal from the FOI regime of records which are currently potentially accessible is a retrograde step, especially in the absence of evidence that the existing exemption provisions are not sufficiently robust to allow the refusal of access where this is justified. One can only wonder at the governance arrangements that permit this piecemeal and sectional approach to FOI policy which completely ignores the public interest in favour of political and administrative pragmatism.

This approach is not just confined to the FOI Acts. The Ombudsman (Amendment) Bill which is currently before the Oireachtas, among other things, proposes an extension of the Ombudsman's remit to the wider public service including the state agency sector (e.g. the Blood Transfusion Service Board, FÁS, the Food Safety Authority, among others) and the third level education institutes. One could be forgiven for thinking that after 26 years of Ombudsman oversight of government departments, local authorities and the health service, and the public demands for increased accountability by the public service, the case for extending the remit would be seen as entirely logical and rational. Far from it; I am genuinely shocked by the representations made by and on behalf of some public bodies (but not the ones named in this paper) arguing against their inclusion in the Ombudsman's remit. Again let me ask, where lies the public interest in an administration that permits, condones and agrees to accommodate such representations?

And what of the values that are supposed to underpin our public service? There is no doubt that the Irish public service is operating today in a radically changed environment to what it was when my office was established. The vocabulary of public service reform is increasingly taken from the world of business. But it sometimes concerns me that, in the midst of this change, we may lose sight of some of the fundamental values which have informed our public service since the creation of the State, values which, in many important respects, are at odds with the values of business. They have to do with fairness, equality, integrity, and a recognition of the notion of the common good. Efficiency and cost-effectiveness are, of course, key elements which the public service must pursue, but it must never be forgotten that, unlike his or her counterpart in the private sector, the user of public services seldom has a choice of an alternative competitive supplier. Fair treatment is vital and must not be lost sight of when efficiency measures are being introduced.

In these straitened times, public servants can struggle to meet competing interests of reduced budgets while, at the same time, attempting to meet rising demands for services. Inevitably, it is the budgetary constraints that win out. For example, over the years, my office has seen instances where public bodies have introduced upper age limits to ration grants even though they had no legal authority to do so. We have seen homeless single people refused consideration for housing on the grounds of limited housing stock and the more pressing needs of homeless family units. It may seem reasonable to create such priorities but not when the governing legislation does not, in fact, authorise a public servant to ration resources in this way. We have seen nursing home subventions refused to elderly people on grounds of excessive means but only to discover on further probing of the complainants' circumstances by my office, that the means ought not to have been taken into account in the first place.

We have had considerable success in overturning many of these *ad hoc* approaches. But the economic downturn has presented new challenges for my office. We now see entire schemes being suspended due to lack of funds; a case in point is the Disabled Persons' Grant Scheme in relation to which several local authorities are not accepting any new applications. Meanwhile, I am approached by complainants with genuine need who are denied benefit under the scheme – a scheme which, in legal terms, still exists but has been starved of funds. What am I to do? Clearly, I cannot ignore the difficult budgetary situation faced by all public bodies. But I can and do challenge public bodies to justify their rationale for suspending a particular scheme while leaving other schemes and programmes untouched. In other words, I expect public bodies to demonstrate a rational and fair approach to the determination of competing priorities which focuses on the public interest and not solely on what is administratively convenient or weighted in favour of the interests of the public body in question.

A common thread running through many of the practices I have cited is a failure to recognise and uphold the public interest or the common good. Both of these terms appear in the Irish Constitution. They are frequently cited by politicians of all parties and never more so than at present when we are all called upon to behave in the national economic interest. But what happens when good governance fails at the highest level, when the Oireachtas, or sections of it, cast aside the high-minded rhetoric and acts demonstrably against that public interest?

This particular example of how deficits in our parliamentary and governmental arrangements can be damaging concerns the work of my own office and relates to the special report I mentioned that I laid before the Dáil and Seanad in late December 2009. The report is titled *Lost at Sea* and deals with an investigation I conducted into a complaint from a Donegal family who believed they had been treated unfairly by the Department of Communications, Marine and Natural Resources. The issue in the complaint is rather complex – involving a scheme to restore tonnage to certain fishermen arising from the sinking of fishing vessels at sea during a particular period of time and I need not go into those details here. Suffice to say that, following an exhaustive investigation, I upheld the complaint and recommended redress which, in financial terms, amounted to about €250,000. By the time the investigation was completed, responsibility for the marine area had transferred to the Department of Agriculture, Fisheries and Food and that department refused to accept my recommendation for redress.

What I am concerned about here is what should happen when an Ombudsman recommendation is rejected by the public body concerned. In short, the issue may be put like this: how does the Ombudsman fit into the wider arrangements for government, and how should government act in order to support the Ombudsman in fulfilling her statutory role? It may seem odd to be raising these questions today, 30 years after the passing of the Ombudsman Act 1980, and 26 years after the setting up of the Ombudsman office: but, in fact, this type of situation has arisen only once before in all of these years and, on that occasion, a solution in the particular case was found eventually. So far, no solution to the present situation has emerged; nor is there clarity as to how, in principle, such situations should be resolved. This means we have to go back to first principles to find a solution which will apply in all such cases in future.

The Ombudsman model followed in Ireland is, essentially, the Scandinavian model. This sees the Ombudsman, who acts in the public interest as part of the overall system of checks and balances, as in some sense representing or protecting the people from any excess or unfairness on the part of government. In this model, the status of the Ombudsman is a key factor; a person of integrity and competence who is given very significant powers to act independently and to adjudicate on complaints about how government operates. In investigating complaints, the Ombudsman acts in an inquisitorial fashion rather than in the adversarial fashion of the courts. The Ombudsman follows the usual rules of constitutional justice/fair procedure. Following an investigation, the Ombudsman makes findings and, where relevant, recommends redress. These recommendations are not legally binding on the public body concerned but come with a very strong persuasive dimension – so much so that it is very rare that an Ombudsman recommendation is rejected. The Ombudsman, for her part, must earn the respect of the public and of government by showing that investigations are conducted fairly, independently and sensibly. It is a measure of the status of the Ombudsman that it is unnecessary to make her recommendations legally binding: in principle, government will want to act on Ombudsman recommendations because the people expect this. Otherwise, in rejecting an Ombudsman recommendation, government will be seen as acting as judge in its own case and as rejecting the need for checks and balances.

And this is the point at which, in the Scandinavian model, parliament enters the picture. The Ombudsman reports to parliament at least annually and, in addition, has access to a parliamentary committee which both scrutinises her work and, where necessary, supports the Ombudsman. In effect, there is a contract of sorts between parliament and the Ombudsman. On the one hand, the Ombudsman goes about her business with independence, integrity and a sense of fairness. On the other hand, while parliament will look carefully at how the Ombudsman conducts her business, and may require the Ombudsman to explain or justify a recommendation or findings, it will generally support the Ombudsman in ensuring that her recommendations are accepted and implemented by government. In this model, parliament does not offer blind support and loyalty to the Ombudsman. While it is predisposed to accepting that the Ombudsman, as an independent statutory office-holder, will have acted properly and reasonably, support in a particular case is likely to follow on from a critical engagement in which any issues relating to the actual case are thrashed out with the Ombudsman.

This, then, is the kind of model on which the Irish Ombudsman's office was expected to operate. And indeed this model of Ombudsman scheme fits well with the model of government set out in the Constitution. Our Constitution envisages a parliamentary democracy operating on the basis of the traditional division of powers between the legislature, executive and judiciary; it envisages the executive power of the State as exercisable by or on the authority of the government, which acts collectively and which is 'responsible to Dáil Éireann'. This model of government, therefore, is posited on notions of checks and balances and accountability. And above all, it is the function of parliament to act as a check on the government and to ensure that it is held to account and is not allowed to act in an arbitrary fashion.

Unfortunately, the model of government set out in the Irish Constitution has become more of a fiction than a reality. In practice the Dáil, and to a slightly lesser extent the Seanad, is controlled very firmly by the government parties through the operation of the whip system. For all practical purposes, and I very much regret having to say this so bluntly, parliament in Ireland has been side-lined and is no longer in a position to hold the executive to account. With the exception of the election of a Taoiseach, almost all decisions of importance are taken by the executive and are rubber-stamped by parliament.

This state of affairs must be deeply frustrating for Oireachtas members themselves who, for the most part, are required to vote on a predetermined basis. Often, I imagine, TDs in particular are forced to exercise a form of 'mental reservation' which takes a considerable toll on them personally.

On the other hand, some members of the Oireachtas would seem no longer conscious that parliament is intended to call the executive to account. This reality was brought home to me while listening recently to RTÉ Radio One's *News at One* programme. Seán O'Rourke asked a government backbencher for his views on the expected Cabinet re-shuffle; various names were men-

tioned for promotion or demotion and the fate of the current
Minister for Health & Children cropped up. The backbencher
was unhappy that the current Minister has (as he saw it) become
unaccountable. The reason why he was taking this view is quite
revealing. It's not because the Minister is failing to explain her-
self in the Dáil or to reply to PQs; the problem, as he saw it, is
that the Minister as an independent TD is not a member of the
main government party and she does not attend party meetings
where she can be questioned by backbenchers. Accountability,
in this model, happens in the party rooms and not in the Dáil. It
was clear from the interview that the idea of the Minister being
held to account within the Dáil or Seanad, by members of any
party, was not an issue. This is not how *Bunreacht na hÉireann*
envisages that parliament will operate.

Both I, and my predecessor Kevin Murphy, have spoken and
written on numerous occasions of the dangers inherent in accepting that parliament is, for the greater part, a charade, that
parliamentarians have in many cases lost the sense of parliament as an independent entity acting in the public interest.
While few will acknowledge this openly, senior civil servants
working with Ministers and sitting in on Oireachtas debates
must, in very many instances, become profoundly cynical; either
that, or they too have lost the sense that a properly functioning
parliament is fundamental to a properly functioning democracy.

I am acutely conscious that, in making these remarks, I may
be accused of petulance or of abusing my position. Yet I suspect
that very many of our elected representatives accept this analysis totally. I recall that in February 2001, the current Minister for
Finance spoke in the Dáil at considerable length, in a debate on
my predecessor's report on Nursing Home Subventions. Mr
Lenihan focused on those aspects of that report which dealt with
the relationship between the Executive and the Legislature; my
predecessor's comments were in the same vein as my own comments here today. Mr Lenihan appeared not to dispute any of
the then Ombudsman's observations and he (Mr Lenihan) went
on to say:

> The Ombudsman's opinion is that in the longer term, the re-
> lationship between the Oireachtas and the Executive, as well

as the relationships within the Executive may need to be thought through afresh in the context of a wider programme of constitutional reform. The All-Party Oireachtas Committee on the Constitution shares this view and it is at present carrying out a study of these issues. Clearly the Ombudsman's report is a graphic example of the pressing need for effective oversight of government and public administration. For a small country like Ireland, the committee is well aware of the need to ensure the government has the capacity to respond speedily to challenges in the external environment. Too sensitive a balance could lead to an enfeebled Executive. We will be discussing this issue at our next meeting. I know the Ombudsman's report will be a valuable contribution to this study.

In the intervening nine years, unfortunately, the scale of the problem has increased rather than decreased. I do think, and again I say this with genuine deference to all the members of the Dáil and Seanad, that the situation is now so serious that it cannot continue to be ignored. It seems to me that a properly functioning parliament is even more necessary at times like these when, in effect, we have a national emergency on our hands.

On 14 December 2009, I laid a report before the Dáil and Seanad in relation to the Lost at Sea case. Despite very extensive correspondence and meetings, the relevant department had refused to implement my recommendation for redress. In these circumstances, my only recourse was to report on this to the Dáil and Seanad and to ask that the Houses would 'take whatever action they deem appropriate in the circumstances'.

The Ombudsman Act does not prescribe what should happen when an Ombudsman recommendation is rejected by a public body. This is not necessarily a problem; many aspects of how the Ombudsman functions are not prescribed in law. Based on the Ombudsman model adopted here in 1980, one would expect that parliament would refer my report to an appropriate committee; that the committee would scrutinise my report in some detail; that as part of that scrutiny, the committee would invite myself and key personnel from the relevant department to appear before it; and, following this engagement, the committee would decide on whether or not to ask the relevant Minister to accept my recommendation and implement it. One would then expect the relevant Minister to heed the conclusion reached by the committee. This is no more than is envisaged in the Scandinavian model of how a state ombudsman scheme should work.

To be absolutely straight, on the basis of this process I would expect a parliamentary committee to reach the conclusion that my recommendation should be accepted and implemented. The whole point in having an ombudsman is that complaints are investigated by an independent, experienced, professional and authoritative office; logically, except when an investigation of equivalent weight is conducted elsewhere, or unless the investigation is shown to have somehow erred in law, then the investigation findings and recommendations should be accepted. As my colleague Ann Abraham, the UK Parliamentary Ombudsman, said last year, speaking to a House of Commons Select Committee: 'Unless the Ombudsman has gone off her trolley, let us leave the findings undisturbed.'

What actually happened was as follows. On 4 February 2010 my Report was the subject of discussion in the Dáil; an attempt to have it referred for consideration by a committee was defeated following a vote on the Order of Business; the vote was 68 to 63 with the Members voting along party lines. On that same day there was a lengthy debate on the Report in the Dáil itself but this took the form of a series of statements rather than any detailed engagement with the substance of the investigation. This process was repeated in the Seanad on 18 February with another exchange of statements. Throughout these exchanges, the Minister of State at the Department of Agriculture, Fisheries and Food expressed the view that, despite his admiration for the work of my office and for the ombudsman institution generally, in this particular case he takes the view that 'there is no basis for payment in the amount proposed or any amount'. Furthermore, the Minister for State rejected my findings that the actions complained of were 'contrary to fair or sound administration'.

On 2 March 2010 the Opposition parties in the Dáil made another attempt to have my Report referred for consideration by an Oireachtas Committee but the Taoiseach took the view that it was a matter for the particular committee as to whether or not it looked at my Report. On 3 March, an attempt was made at a meeting of the Joint Committee on Agriculture, Fisheries and Food to have the Report considered. This attempt failed following a vote which followed party political lines. And there, it appears, matters rest.

I very much appreciate the efforts of those within the Dáil and Seanad who sought to have my Report dealt with, through a Committee, in a manner which is respectful both of the Oireachtas itself and of my office. It is very unfortunate that these efforts followed party lines and could be portrayed as the usual party political jostling which tends to be a feature of parliaments generally. Those who wished to have the matter dealt with in Committee were seeking no more than is expected from the Ombudsman model adopted in this country in 1980.

Through the operation of the whip system, both in the Dáil, Seanad and in Committee, the Executive has spancelled the Oireachtas and prevented the Houses, by way of a Committee, from dealing with the Report. By preventing the Oireachtas from dealing with the Report, the government parties have brought about a situation in which the government has been able to act as the judge in its own case. The saga began with maladministration and has ended, to date at least, with poor governance.

It is possible that the government's response in this case is a 'one off' prompted, as many observers have suggested, by a sense of loyalty to a colleague, the former Minister for the Marine and Natural Resources, who devised the scheme along with his officials, following representations from constituents and others and against the initial advice of his department officials. The gentleman who complained to me when he was refused access to the scheme had had no inside track, and the tragic details of his particular case lay unfound within the filing cabinets of the department. I cannot say if what the observers suggest is actually the case but I note again the mismatch of rhetoric and action. The last Financial Regulator was excoriated for not doing his job adequately, for allowing himself to be captured by the system he was supposed to monitor, by not rooting out maladministration in the banking system and thus failing to serve the public interest. My office has done – in its area of responsibility – precisely what the Financial Regulator was accused of not doing in his. And the result is as I have outlined.

I will quote once again Minster Dempsey:

> The most important part of the job (of public representative) is ensuring, through our work, that the system works for every citizen, not just the ones who come to our clinics. Public representatives shouldn't be distracted from their national function by constant clientilism – by becoming a hero to one citizen through finding a way around a system when the real responsibility is to change the system to benefit all citizens ... Any time public representatives abandon their judgement to serve a lobby group they don't believe in, they are betraying their calling. Our state and semi-state organisations are not scrutinised nearly enough by our national politicians, particularly in relation to their service delivery to citizens. Because the whole basis of what we do politically is adversarial competition, there's little opportunity for a collective approach to solving problems.

Indeed ...

Let me also quote from another leader, this time from business, the former head of Unilever, Niall Fitzgerald, interviewed recently in the *Irish Times*. Talking about the lack of true independence in many of Ireland's boardrooms, he said that the lack of adequate regulation was not the problem.

'The thing that really worries me,' he said, 'if I was losing sleep about it on behalf of Ireland, is that there are too many people who have a vested interest in there being no accountability. If the leaders of a society are not prepared to hold themselves accountable, or there are not the institutions which are sufficiently independent to hold them accountable, then I think you have a very serious problem on your hands.'

To conclude:
- acting in the public interest is the cornerstone of democracy;
- in looking at the nuts and bolts of government, as the OECD has done and as is envisaged in the government's Transforming Public Service Programme, it is essential to confront also problems at the high end of government, that is, how parliament operates;

- tinkering with the nuts and bolts of government, in the absence of reforming our parliament, is not enough; it is to overlook the elephant in the corner;
- a modest proposal for parliamentary reform would be for the main political parties to agree to relax the very rigid party discipline now there and to accept that TDs should have some freedom to follow the dictates of their own conscience;
- as regards my immediate difficulty as Ombudsman, arising from the Lost at Sea case, I would hope that the Oireachtas will find a mechanism to allow the matter be dealt with in a calm and reasonable fashion and in accordance with the model of Ombudsman which, certainly as I understand it, was the intention of the legislature in 1980 when it passed the Ombudsman Act of that year.

CHAPTER THREE

Community Development
Reimagining Community Development for our Time

Fr Harry Bohan

Community Development has a long history in Ireland, but was known by other names. It was central to Irish rural life. To a large extent it was informal, but very much part of the social and economic fabric of life when times were poor and money was scarce. People shared their labour. It was known as the *meitheal* when work had to be done. The social aspect of it was known as *cooring*. Both were essential for the development of the community. Through the *meitheal* the work was done and through *cooring* local affairs were discussed. Put another way – the family, extended family, neighbourhood, townland and parish were the systems within which generations of Irish people were held together. These were the generations of people who survived the famine and stayed at home. They were the generations who were part of an Ireland that experienced the revivalist movements of the 1880s, such as the GAA, the Gaelic League and religious revivalism, the co-operative movement of the 1890s and 1900s, the Easter Rising of 1916, Independence and Civil War of the 1920s, economic war of the 1930s, rationing of the 1940s, mass emigration of the 1950s. They were the generations who were part of the new Ireland in the 1960s – the Industrial, Communications, Education and Vatican II revolutions – the oil crisis 1970s, recession 1980s, and Celtic Tiger 1994-2007.

This brief sketch underlines the fact that up to the 1960s life for many was about survival. During most of this time what we call community development was, for the most part, informal. Organisations such as Muintir na Tíre, Macra na Feirme, the ICA and others emerged during the first half of the century, all on a voluntary basis. From the 1960s onwards, Irish society became more organisationally focused and so did community development.

Since 1958 Irish society has been busy constructing an economy, and for very good reasons. Prior to this, emigration had drained the life-blood from the community, with 50,000 people being forced to leave each year during the 1950s. Prior to that again, we had the decades which could be described as a period in the aftermath of a famine which left an indelible mark on generations of Irish people. It had a traumatic effect on the Irish psyche. The country lost half of its population in a few decades. The experience reverberated long after food was available again in steady supply.

So, basic survival was a good reason why people would share with one another their time and talents.

Another reason for people to be together was as a buffer to powerful influences from outside. The 20th century opened with colonialism, was then dominated by clericalism and ended with capitalism. During most of this time, community action was in many ways the one great buffer to the excesses or dominance of any one influence.

The concept of community development is also significant then and now as an expression of self, the civic self. It is an important expression of citizenship. The involvement of the self in community whether for idealism, functional reasons, or in giving a person a sense of solidarity, leads to a building of relationship with neighbours and with the wider community. This was particularly true at a time when government influence on people's lives was nothing like what it came to be in the second half of the century.

Voluntarism is central to the concept of community development. However, for it to work effectively, a close relationship between the statutory and voluntary is essential. This happens in a diverse way in Ireland. The community or voluntary sector now comprises organisations ranging from voluntary hospitals, schools, sports organisations, associations dealing with social services, environmental organisations, tenant's rights, Traveller's rights, rural development organisations and housing associations. The sector is rarely, if ever, thought of in economic terms. Over 10 years ago, it was reckoned these organisations spent a total of €4.2 billion in cash terms – more than agriculture and fishing which spent €3.62 billion and almost twice as much

as public administration and defence which spent €2.22 billion.[1]
It hasn't been seen in this way because it has been associated
with goodness.

This association with doing good can mean the sector's importance is only perceived as occurring at a level on a par with
things that are immeasurable. However, when focusing on the
sector from an economic viewpoint one can get a very different
picture. This is a point that needs to be emphasised in relation to
what is now known as 'the third sector' i.e. the community and
voluntary sector. As state and semi-state organisations (popul-
arly known as 'quangos') multiplied, the voluntary sector tended
to be marginalised and regarded as 'do-goodery'. The real work
was now going to be carried out by these bodies and highly paid
executives within them. This has resulted in undermining the
community development concept and at an enormous financial
cost to the taxpayer.

New Era
In the mid 1990s, Ireland became part of a global market economy.
Almost overnight we became the best fed, best housed, best
educated, most employed generation ever to have lived in
Ireland. Side by side with this major growth in the economy we
witnessed an equally significant disengagement by much of the
population from the supports and institutions that sustained
them for generations. During these years – 1994-2007 – the period
of the Celtic Tiger, we experienced serious disconnection from
family and community.

Institutions which shaped us were finding it difficult to address a youthful and questioning culture. Exposure to the global
culture was intensive. We moved into an economic system that
focused on 'wants' more than 'needs'. Wants are driven by marketing. They are about 'keeping up with the Jones's' and very
quickly breathe a culture of borrowing and indebtedness. They
suggest that people don't need people any more. They strip
away the idea of saving. They fixate people on 'things' and they
lead them into massive borrowings and impossible debt in
acquiring these things. They remove people from the local and
towards the global and the concept of globalisation.

1. Donoghue *et al* (1999)

In short, globalisation, meaning easy movement of ideas, trade and people across the world, became a significant force. We no longer easily identified with the people, places, or structures that gave previous generations an identity and a feeling of belonging. And we know that life without commitment means life without responsibility to others or for others. The independent life leads to isolation and is the recipe for a very privatised society. Is it an exaggeration to suggest that we reached a stage when neighbours would not be aware or even care if we were to disappear from among them? As often as not, 'neighbour' has come to mean someone with a common address but little more.

The reality is that the market economy does not function as a community. It is a highly competitive environment as distinct from one that depends on relationships. We have invested huge resources in developing the economy. We are now challenged to make a clear distinction between market values and social values, or at least to balance them. We are challenged to reflect on values that will reconnect us, which will value life and relationships.

We don't need reminding that Ireland, together with other parts of the western world, has been dealt some damaging blows in recent times. This bursting of the property bubble and the collapse of confidence in the banking system have left a crisis of confidence in institutions. We are living through a period of great upheaval. Scandals in the church, business, banks, broken promises in politics and breaches of trust, have all led to top/down, command/control type leadership being called into serious question. To where and to whom do people turn to sort out the mess?

The problems facing our society now are very different to anything we faced in the past. In a sense we have nothing in history to guide us and no language to articulate it. We have come a long way in terms of economic and social development but more particularly in terms of the cultural diversity that now characterises the country. Some of the change has been positive and some has been negative, but it has all been momentous. As we look forward, it is clear that the change that has occurred to date is only the tip of the iceberg.

We are certainly at the point where power and authority

have been seriously undermined, with the church, business, and the political firmament all having suffered serious reputational damage. Having seen the 'pillars of authority' dismantled, there is now a sense of vacuum that could lead either way.

Direction for the future
In which direction will our society evolve? This has to be the key challenge for the future. We have identified that we are coming from a period dominated by globalisation. We agree that a sense of belonging has weakened and personal freedom increased. This, in turn, has led to extreme individualism, but it could also give rise to a deeper search for community and belonging. As the shock of the crises recedes, many are looking to people on the ground for solutions. For example, more and more Catholics are turning to their local church for solutions and they are beginning to take ownership of their church. The concept of community is again becoming central to both social and economic life at local level.

The fact is that nature does not like a vacuum. But a vacuum is what occurs when people demand freedom without accepting responsibility. A question we all need to ask now is, 'Is the future my responsibility?' We had a powerful tradition of community living at a time when survival was all that mattered. The family and community bond held generations together – all of this in times of poverty. Can those same systems become central to finding our way into the future?

I, in my life and experiences, have come to believe that people are searching for connections and if facilitated to make these they will respond. I have also come to believe that leaders in society are not sufficiently aware of the changing face of society in terms of what isolation, individualism and independency have been doing. There are clear indications that many people are conscious that they can no longer live isolated from others. The naked fact is that we are all interdependent. There seems to be a new cry for togetherness, even in the midst of affluence or the 'appearances' of it. A new order is called for. So, where do we begin? Could it be with a new type of leadership; one which facilitates participation and values the place where everyone belongs?

Two concerns now lie at the heart of democracies – discontent and even anger. One is the fear that, individually and collectively, we are losing control of the forces that govern our lives. The other is the sense that, from family to neighbourhood to nation, the moral fabric of community was seriously unravelled during the Celtic Tiger years. These two fears – the loss of self-government and the erosion of community – together define the anxiety that the prevailing agenda has failed to answer or even address.

Our view of progress has been one of climbing the ladders of knowledge and power. It has been about competition – competing with others for more and more status, wealth and power. Its offer of meaning for life and living has been about these rather than inner contentment and meaningful relationships.

But these values are beginning to be questioned. It is no longer good enough for economic policy simply to create wealth at the expense of the environment or people in the third world or poor people who are homeless, or people who find no meaning to life anymore. Organisations such as the World Bank, the International Monetary Fund and World Health Organisation, are all shifting from a purposeless approach to economic policy to one which has a purpose. And growing numbers of people are emphasising the importance of values in shaping our future – values such as truth, participation, social responsibility, a sense of the sacred. In all of this there is emerging a new vision of progress – one which is developmental, one which gives value and meaning to our lives. It will be about developing our own potential, enabling other people to do the same, and contributing to the development of our society.

This might be known as a 21st century definition of community development and presents a major challenge to finding a new definition of leadership and a new way of being leader whether in business, government or any other organisation. It also presents major challenges to enable people to take responsibility.

Direction for the future will depend very much on identifying a new vision of leadership. It is clear now that leadership of the future has to be value based. The market value without the support and influence of more noble ideals lead to self and sectional interests. Institutions and organisations will have to return to first beginnings. What are banks for? What is the church for? How does business and community connect? Is politics about parties or people? To whom do young people turn for ideals and for a sense of meaning and purpose? What is the role of the local in the future? What kind of community/local leadership is needed if people are to participate, be creative, develop local resources, be environmentally conscious, and have a serious sense of responsibility?

Values such as trust, truth, caring, participation, responsibility and spirituality are all required as a matter of honour and decency in any civilised society. They may sound aspirational, philosophical and impractical within systems and organisations that foster the culture of pragmatism and hard-headedness, but they are an integral part of the leadership of the future.

It is worth repeating that the recovery that is needed cannot be just a repetition of the past. We live at a time that proves Einstein right: 'No problem can be solved from the same level of thinking that created it.' Restoring the balance between local and global is now essential. Act locally – think globally, is more relevant than ever.

Community development of the future will depend then on a new vision of leadership. It will involve sharing power and authority, building collaborative relationships, bringing people on board and allowing them personal investment and ownership. It will involve the development of a participative leadership which involves people and gives them a stake in the decisions that affect their lives. Participation releases creativity, it encourages people to use their own ingenuity in solving problems. People show greater commitment to action when they have been involved in the decision-making process. A participative leadership style promotes co-operation and collaboration rather than competition. Working on shared goals enhances social commitment as people are more committed to each other.

The Céifin Conference of 2009, titled 'Who's in Charge: Towards a Leadership of Service',[2] focused on the fact that the styles of leadership we have inherited simply have not worked in our time. It is obvious now that top/down leadership will not

2. Bohan (2010)

work in the future. This was a key message running through the conference.

For example:

Philip Lowe, in his keynote speech, 'Private Enterprise; Public Values and Civic Responsibilities', outlined how the banking crisis and the loss of trust and confidence in the financial/banking system on which a market economy so depends, came about. He asked: 'Isn't it time to look beyond regulation to some form of contractualisation of the relationship between banks and the rest of society? … Shouldn't there be in the end recognition by the financial sector of some civic responsibilities which go along with the freedom they have to create value for their shareholders?'

Ray Kinsella addressed the topic under the heading 'Re-imagining Community: the Céifin revolution of 2009'. He suggested that a reconnection to our spiritual heritage provides an anchor for Ireland at this time and that we need a leadership of service, with a vision that will point the way to re-imagining community.

Paula Downey suggested that 'most of the institutions of our time have completely lost their way because they have forgotten their founding ethic'. She called for 'a new leadership agenda to transform our wider social culture by transforming the culture of the institutions that shape it'.

Dearbhail McDonald, in her paper 'Re-imagining Political Leadership,' said: 'We need a far reaching vision of the sort of society we want to be when this crisis passes … Nothing short of a revolution in our political culture and our collective attitude towards serving others will stop the rot that has corroded what has always been a noble calling'.

The common thread running through this conference was the urgent need to re-imagine and redefine community development for our time. If trust is to be restored, people will have to be facilitated to take responsibility for their future. In other words, the concept of community development will have to take on a whole new meaning.

References:

Bohan, H., (ed) (2010), *Who's in Charge? – Towards a Leadership of Service* (Céifin Papers 2009), Veritas.

Donoghue, F., Anheier, H. K. and Salamon, L. M., (1999), *Uncovering the Nonprofit Sector in Ireland: Its Economic Value and Significance*, Dublin: National College of Ireland.

CHAPTER FOUR

Health
The Health Wealth Divide: There is an Alternative

Sara Burke

Introduction: Health and wealth

We know that poor people get sick more often and die younger. We know that investing in public health now saves money and lives in the future. We know that the two-tier nature of Irish public hospitals is divisive and privileges private patients over public patients. Yet in the decade when we had most, despite endless restructuring and 'reform', the government failed to adopt policies which could more evenly distribute wealth and create a quality, universal health system.

In fact the PD/Fianna Fáil/Green government in power since 1997 did the very opposite. They introduced tax and welfare policies in favour of the wealthy. Government policies increased inequalities in health and wealth and further institutionalised the two-tier system of public hospital care. Simultaneously, they drove down the tax base so that by 2010 the investments made in the health system over the previous decade were no longer sustainable. As a direct result, significant cuts were introduced across health and social care services – cuts which will be felt by patients and the public for years to come).[1] From the HSE's own figures, there were 3,016 fewer staff in December 2009 than there were in September 2007.[2]

Broader economic policies are being dealt with elsewhere in this book, but it is simply not possible to write a chapter about health in Ireland without drawing attention to the fact that while life expectancy has improved in the decade of the boom, the inequalities that exist between rich and poor have been maintained and in some instances have increased as a result of regressive fiscal and economic policies.

Some recent analysis of the budgetary measures introduced

1. Burke (2009)
2. HSE (2010)

since the economic crisis raised its menacing head, claim that these budgetary measures are progressive, hitting those on highest incomes most. However, when one scratches the surface of assumptions upon which such assessments are based, one realises they fail to take into account certain important factors. For example, in the budget of April 2009, the government withdrew the Christmas bonus from social welfare recipients. For a single person who was on €204 a week, this was in effect a 2% cut in income. Then in December 2009, the budget cut social welfare payments by €4% – these two measures combined reduced the income of those on the lowest income by 6%. Yet because this drop in income for those on social welfare was not factored into the economic model, the budgetary measures were deemed progressive.

The international and national evidence is quite clear that income inequalities are directly related to health inequalities, that lowering the income of those on the lowest incomes will increase inequalities in health and death rates of the poorest.[3] Kate Pickett and Richard Wilkinson have expertly gathered the evidence that there is more crime, more imprisonment, higher rates of mental illness, illiteracy, murder and obesity in more unequal societies. They show that inequality, no matter what way it is measured, is not just bad for those at the bottom, but is important to the vast majority of the population, and that quite simply inequality is bad for nearly everyone. Conversely, they prove that societies which have more equal distribution of health and wealth are beneficial to everyone.[4] For example, if you are middle class in Sweden you will be healthier and live a longer life than if you are middle class in Ireland, where inequalities of income and health are significantly higher.

The model of economic development that created Ireland's boom and bust was one based on the assumption that, in the words of the then Minister for Justice, Equality and Law Reform, Michael McDowell, 'inequality was inevitable'. Explaining this in an interview with the *Economist* magazine in Autumn 2004, McDowell said that 'inequality is an inevitable part of the society of incentives that Ireland, thankfully, has become'.

3. Marmot (2009)
4. Pickett and Wilkinson (2009)

And Michael McDowell was right in his assessment that in-equality was a natural outcome of the PD/Fianna Fáil neo-liberal economic orthodoxy that prevailed then and now. What he failed to point out is that other competitive states have adopted economic models that are more progressive in their nature and that purposefully value social, welfare and well-being outcomes as well as economic ones.[5]

If Ireland is to be a republic where wealth and health are based on the principle of equality and are more evenly distrib-uted, then a radical change in our economic model is required.

The health system

And what of our health system? The Irish health system is the focus of much public and political criticism. It is portrayed as a system in crisis; chronic queues of trolleys in emergency depart-ments; long waiting times for outpatient appointments for pub-lic patients; poor hospital hygiene; what often seems like a con-tinuous stream of health scandals in the midst of the boom. And while there has been a disproportionate amount of catastrophes and bottlenecks in the Irish system, many people receive quality care day in, day out from front line health and social care providers.

Also, whether it is local campaigns to save hospitals or long waits or poor quality care, the focus is disproportionately on hospitals. Yet most health and social care is best delivered out-side of the hospital environment. And while there has been a concerted effort led by Health Service Executive CEO Brendan Drumm to re-orient our services to primary and community care, this rhetoric has been slowly followed by action. Simultaneous to the slow progress on primary and community care, these communities witness the downgrading of their local hospitals. As a result of these factors, there is a complete discon-nect between the people who run and plan the health system with people's everyday experience of it. Central to this has been an eradication of trust and credibility between the public and those responsible for the health services, especially the Minister for Health, Mary Harney and the senior managers in the HSE.

5. Adshead *et al* (2008)

Health policy

In December 2001, the government published a new health strategy called 'Quality and Fairness – A Health System for You'.[6] The Fianna Fáil/PD coalition had been in power since 1997, the economy was booming but there was increasing discontent with the health service. Under the stewardship of Minister Micheál Martin in health a substantial consultation took place while developing the health strategy. The government went to the country in 2002 saying to the people, re-elect us and we will deliver the 121 commitments in the health strategy. The government was re-elected and pretty much immediately budgets were curtailed to make up for the pre-election spending spree by Minister for Finance, Charlie McCreevy. As a result the health strategy was made instantly redundant, as there was no political will or funding to resource the significant extra services promised in it.

The HSE

What followed the strategy publication was three years of reviewing and reports on what the new health system should look like. In 2004, local politicians were not re-appointed to their local health boards. In January 2005, the Health Service Executive (HSE) came into being, merging the old health boards and a range of other health agencies into one unified executive. Part of the rationale for the HSE was to ensure consistent quality care across the country, as up to 2005 each health board, governed by local politicians, had operated as independent fiefdoms providing different coverage and quality of care in each different region.

The foundation of the HSE resulted in endless restructuring and organising how health and social care services were provided. Local health offices replaced old community care areas, regional areas were established as were hospital networks. Despite the pretence of rationalisation of health services, in particular in administration, under the guise of the new HSE, not one person lost their job.

The HSE was badly planned and poorly led. The legislation to set it up was rushed through the Dáil in what Maev-Ann

---

6. Department of Health (2001)

Wren describes as a 'guillotined debate' without any real time for the Oireachtas to debate and amend as would be the normal practice for such important policy change.[7] It was without a CEO for seven months until August 2005 when Brendan Drumm took on the role.

The detail of this new organisation had been poorly worked out and resulted in increased confusion amongst the public and the staff as to who was responsible for what. Remarkably, front-line services pretty much continued as before. A central criticism of the new HSE was the delayed decision-making processes, with all decisions, even minor ones, having to go 'up the line' to Dublin. The further delay in relaying decisions back down resulted in stymied local responses, disillusioned staff and frustrated patients.

What is most incredible about the development of the health strategy and the HSE is that when there was most opportunity – both political support and economic resources – the provision of a universal health system was never even contemplated. While many outside of government advocated such a system, those in leadership positions in the Department of Health and in government put their energy into restructuring rather than reform, into quality care rather than equitable access, into tweaking the old dysfunctional system rather than creating a brand new, functioning one.

Our complicated, unique mix of public and private health and social care
Incongruously, on the face of it, Ireland has a 'functioning' first world health system accessible to the 'whole population'. Every Irish citizen is entitled to public hospital care with charges for entry in to Emergency Departments (€120) and inpatient hospital care (paid for at a rate of €70 a day and capped at 10 days at €700 maximum paid per year). Neither of these charges include the actual cost of medical care so if you are brought to hospital in an ambulance no charge is applied or if you need a year of cancer treatment, just the ten day fee (€700) will be charged.

In OCED analyses of the Irish health system, Ireland is always

7. Tussing and Wren (2006)

portrayed as 'universal'.[8] However in Ireland in 2010, the final remnant of universalism was removed by the imposition of a prescription charge to medical card holders. The second last aspect of universalism was removed in the first emergency budget in October 2008 when the government took away medical cards from about 30,000 'richer' over 70-year-olds. There are many incomprehensible aspects of the Irish health system but by far the most remarkable is the fact that access to most aspects is based on ability to pay, not need.

About one third of the population qualify for medical cards which entitles them to 'free' access to GPs, public hospitals and (up to summer 2010) prescription items. In June 2010, the government introduced a prescription charge on medical card holders of 50 cent per item with a maximum of €10 per family per month. While this might seem like a small charge to deter excessive drug use and to assist with the growing drugs budget, all the international evidence is to the contrary. It shows that even a small fee puts people off using these drugs; in particular it deters people with chronic conditions including mental illness, from taking their drugs, and raises little revenue. Also, if government is interested in deterring increased prescribing, then it needs to target the doctors who prescribe the drugs, not the patients who take them on their recommendation.

Access to GPs without a charge is an effective pro-poor measure ensuring that people on lower incomes or with poorer health have access to a central component of primary care.[9] 'Free' access to hospital diagnostics, treatment and care is also significant. However, the wait times for diagnostics and outpatient appointments for public patients are notoriously long, particularly in some specialities such as neurology. Those who opt for and can afford to pay privately can often skip the queue into the public hospital system by paying for the initial outpatient appointment privately.

Uniquely in Ireland we allow and incentivise private, profitable practice in our public hospitals. While the private work is officially limited to 20% of the hospital work load, many hospitals carry out private work well in excess of this, some above

8. OECD (2010)
9. Layte *et al* (2007)

40%. The dual practice of public and private care in public hospitals means that private patients can often get diagnosis, treatment and care quicker too. In effect, Irish health policy actively discriminates against half the population, who cannot afford private care, who happen to be the poorer and sicker in Irish society – an extraordinary position for a republic that has equity as one of the principles of its own health strategy.

Two thirds of the population have no medical card and have to pay out of pocket each time they access aspects of the health system. The majority of the population without medical cards pay a fee each time they visit their GP, between €40 and €60, with price often depending on the location of the GP. They also pay for drug costs up to €120 per month.

About half the population has private health insurance which covers the cost of most inpatient hospital care but usually those who opt for private care pay each time they see a consultant on an outpatient basis. Every citizen is entitled to the public hospital care as outlined above, however many are motivated to have private health insurance not just to cover the cost of inpatient private care but to ensure quicker access to diagnosis and treatment. It is the 15-20% of the population who have neither medical cards nor private health insurance who fare worst in the Irish health system, with no access to free care, nor any of the privileges of faster access that private health insurance can provide.

When it comes to a range of allied health professionals, access is often based on luck or location rather than clear entitlements. Under the 1970 health act, entitlements are unclear. For example, are older people who are not medical card holders entitled to public health nurses? Technically, they are not. But in effect, many receive such services as decisions are discretionary. However, many people pay privately for services such as occupational therapy, physiotherapy and speech and language therapy. Even if these services exist at a local level within the public health services and you are entitled to them, the waiting lists are so long that people end up buying care from private providers.

The 2001 health strategy committed to reviewing eligibility for Irish health services. Nine years on this review is still 'ongoing'. The Department of Health say they will put recommendations to government in 2010 after the Expert Group on Resource

Allocation reports to the Minister. Part of the public dissatisfaction with the Irish health system is this continued confusion about who is entitled to what (and indeed who is responsible for what). Is it an accident that there has been no clarification from government in the last nine years on this particular issue? Does it suit the powers that be that this issue is constantly avoided and obfuscated?

In the opinion of this author, one of the many crimes of the boom was not to introduce a universal health system where access is based on need not ability to pay, where there is an even playing field for all Irish citizens when it comes to health and social care. The opportunity of the bust, or the economic crisis, is to radically rethink what type of society we want to live in, and what type of services we want to provide.

Canadian President Trudeau in the 1970s said that a health system should be based on the principle of the 'healthy and wealthy paying for unhealthy and the unwealthy' – recognising that we will all be unhealthy (even if not unwealthy) at some stage in our life, and advocating a solidarity model of paying and providing care.

It is essential that the lack of clarity on who is entitled to what is addressed in Ireland. The problem with this happening under the current Fianna Fáil/Green regime with an ex-PD as Minister for Health is that the chances are there will be a further retrenchment of entitlement. In contrast, all the opposition parties (even the Green party who are happy to coalesce with the current divisive health policy) are committed to universal health care provided on the basis of need, not ability to pay.

Universal health care
This is the first time in the history of this country that the majority of political party support has taken a position in favour of universal health care. A change in government coinciding with the consideration of eligibility should lead to the adoption of universalism in Irish health care. The exact nature of it will depend significantly on what combination of political parties is in power, on who is the Minister for Health, alongside pragmatic issues such as funding and the capacity of the system to embark on such change.

This momentum for universal health care is fundamentally an ideological shift away from the Poor Law politics and health care provision – where a minimum service was provided for the poorest and the rest had to pay for care – to a system of quality universal health care in which all citizens access care on an equitable basis. Of course the wealthy and the privileged may insist on paying for additional luxuries such as a single room or hotel facilities but ultimately each citizen, no matter what their wealth or class, is entitled to timely access to the same quality services. While this is the norm in most other European countries, it has never been the norm here. If the opposition political parties are to be believed, such a position is not so far away as it seems right now.

Once the political and ideological steps have been taken to achieve this outcome, then comes the nitty gritty of trying to decide the best way to achieve it and to do so in a way and time-frame that brings and keeps citizens on board. This is no small feat. Only then, could we even begin to think of ourselves as a republic, where healthcare is a right, not a privilege.

There is much work being done on the introduction of a social health insurance model to Ireland. The Adelaide Hospital Society has commissioned a series of reports from the Health Policy and Management Department in Trinity College Dublin on the possibilities, the models, the cost and the steps required to introduce social health insurance in Ireland.[10] This work in itself has informed the debate and the growing consensus on such a model. Central to its introduction is increased investment and the building up of the capacity of the system as it currently exists.

Across the board, the Irish health system has fewer doctors, health service staff, buildings, beds, and community health facilities than our European contemporaries. In order to be able effectively to introduce social health insurance (or any form of universal health care), there needs to be significant expansion of current services. Such expansion is required no matter what type of financing mechanism is adopted. The case could equally be argued that given where we stand, we would be better delivering a universal system based on a tax rather than social insurance model.

10. Thomas *et al* (2010)

But no matter what type of model is adopted, if and when we go down the universal healthcare route – which is the only way forward – we will need to spend more on our health and social services than we do now. Also we could spend much of what we are spending in a different way. For example, if all the money paid out-of-pocket for medical expenses and treatment were instead paid through taxes or a health insurance model, it may be a more effective and efficient way to provide free, universal access to health care.

Currently doctors and hospitals are paid differently for the treatment and care of public and private patients. They are paid salaries and lump sums for public patients no matter how many they treat, regardless of the quality of care and are paid a fee for service each time they treat a private patient. Ask any economist, economic incentives matter. The main economic incentive in the Irish public hospital system is to treat more private patients quicker.

When there is political and public consensus that we want really good quality healthcare for all, then we need to pay for it. Ireland's level of social spending is still well below European averages no matter what measurement is used and in the last year of comparative figures (at the height of the boom) we were just hitting the OECD average of health spend, making up for decades of under spend.[11]

Diverting public money into private care
Another anomaly in the Irish health system is the disproportionate spend of public money on private, largely for-profit healthcare. This money comes out of the public purse and diverts much needed money away from public health service provision. For example, up to 80% of the care of a private patient in a public hospital is subsidised by public money.[12] While consultants are paid privately for their private work in public hospitals, many other aspects of the patient's care are paid for out of public money, such as nursing, theatre time and equipment.

Also those with private health insurance get tax breaks. As part of the pro-rich incentives that were put in place by the

11. OECD (2009)
12. Thomas *et al* (2006)

PD/Fianna Fáil government in the late 1990s and subsequent years, tax breaks were given to developers to build private for-profit nursing homes, health clinics and hospitals wherever they wanted and without any form of regulation and quality control. As a direct result of Charlie McCreevy's changes to the Finance Act in 2001 and 2002, by 2008, one in three hospital beds and two in three nursing home beds were in the private for-profit sector.

While there was always a mix of public and private care in Ireland, up to 2000 the private care was largely provided by voluntary not-for-profit providers, often through the religious orders. But what we have seen in the last ten years as a direct result of government policy is the marketisation of healthcare, the entry and in some aspects of care, the dominance of a private model which is neither publicly accessible nor consistent with public health policy.

The cancer strategy is a case in point. Under the determined leadership of Minister Mary Harney and Professor Tom Keane, who managed the cancer control programme, cancer care was successfully transferred from thirty hospitals to eight between 2007 and 2009. Despite much public and political opposition it happened. This policy was pursued on the basis that patient care is better if there is a higher volume of patients and a greater critical mass of experts who are dealing with such cases on a daily basis. This makes sense from both a quality of care perspective and an economic one – it is just not possible to staff thirty hospitals at an adequate level to make cancer care safe, let alone of high quality. There are ongoing issues for patients in the north west due to the distance that patients from Donegal have to travel for treatment in Galway. However, for the most part this argument has been won; most cancer care happens in the eight centres and the vast majority of people are willing to travel for such care. However, when we look at private provision, the direct opposite is happening with many small private hospitals offering cancer treatment, outside of and contrary to the national cancer control policy.

The same contradictory policy is seen in the National Treatment Purchase Fund (NTPF). After the election in 2002, when the new health strategy became redundant due to the absence of funding and political will to implement it, one of the few actions that was followed up on was the establishment of the NTPF. Initially, it was given a budget of €5 million which multiplied twenty fold in seven years. Notably, no other part of the public health system experienced a twenty fold increase in funding during the same time period. The role of the fund is to buy private care, mostly in private hospitals, for public patients as a way to bring down long waits for public patients. While the longer waits have largely been eradicated for treatment, the government's 2001 target that 'no public patient will wait longer than three months for treatment following referral from an out-patient department by the end of 2004' remains far from achieved.

The NTPF annual report for 2009, published in April 2010, shows that over 18,500 adults and children were waiting more than three months for treatment in December 2009.[13] While many people receive quicker treatment through the fund, it has failed spectacularly to eradicate waiting lists, let alone reach the nine-year-old target. Meanwhile, it has diverted hundreds of millions of public money away from the public system into the private, for-profit health providers, and the problems which cause the long waits in the public system persist.

In conclusion
The last ten years saw a quadrupling of the health budget, a 61% increase in staffing, and expansion of some aspects of the public health system. But this all happened amidst a baby boom, a growing older population with increased health care needs and more expensive treatments for patients. Since 2007, there has been a moratorium on staff, a drive for efficiencies to do more with fewer staff, and since 2009 a lower budget and a transfer of payment from the State to the patient. This combined with rising expectations and demands, efforts to improve and standardise quality of care, as well as significant privatisation of many aspects of care, paints a complicated picture of health and social care in Ireland at present.

What is most evident from the Irish healthcare landscape

---

13. NTPF (2010)

over the last ten years is the failure to really reform – to provide quality universal healthcare for all our citizens, and to redistribute wealth in favour of the health of all. Instead, the health services experienced a myriad of restructuring and reorganisation – most of which remained unapparent to the people using the services. While there has been sustained effort to save and reduce inefficiencies, many remain entrenched in the complicated, divisive system of care that is inherent to the Irish model.

And although there has been some progress evident in areas like nurses prescribing drugs, improving quality cancer care, the provision of nearly 12 million home help hours in 2009, such improvements remain invisible to the public at large.

The ingredients for a quality, universal health service for Ireland are more obvious now than at any time since the foundation of the State. Apart from Minister Mary Harney and Fianna Fáil, there is unanimous political support for some sort of universal health care. In order to regain the people's trust in our health system, small but concrete changes need to take place on the road to such a system. This can only be done by continuing to build up and improve the public health system so that people begin to trust and have good experiences of the health services; by reducing waiting times for emergency care and outpatient appointment; by making access to care based on need, not ability to pay – why not start with free care for all under six years of age?; by convincing the public and therefore the politicians that 'we get what we pay for' and if we want universal quality care then we need to pay for it; by removing the inequalities and inefficiencies that are inbuilt in the system; by not putting public money into private, profitable health care.

Crucial to achieving universal, quality health care is leadership. No great social or economic change takes place without a strong, visionary leader. But the most vital component is public momentum – remember the power of the older people in October 2008, who forced the government to make multiple u-turns on their original objective to remove medical cards from over 70-year-olds. While the protests did not stop the government removing the universal entitlement to medical cards, they did result in much government embarrassment which means that many more over 70-year-olds still have medical cards than the government intended. It is much easier to get a medical card if you are over 70 than under 70 as a result of the older people's action.

The government will give the Irish people the health system it wants. In the 1890s, there were many different forms of peoples' movements which helped shape the foundation of the new Irish state. Such a desire for change is palpable now from a myriad of places – from the opposition parties, from civil society, from academia, from the unions, from the community and voluntary sector, from the disparate Left, from this book. These festering ideas and energies need to be harnessed for change – radical change which will bring about a more equitable distribution of health and wealth in Ireland in the decades to come. There is an alternative to the current health wealth divide – let's seize the current crisis to create that alternative.

References:

Adshead, M., Kirby, P. and Millar, M. (2008), *Contesting the State: Lessons from the Irish State*, Manchester: Manchester University Press.

Burke, S. (2009), *Irish Apartheid, Healthcare Inequality in Ireland*, Dublin: New Island.

Burke, S. (2010), *Saving our public health service amidst an economic crisis*. Available from: http://saraburke. wordpress. com/2010/05/07/saving-our-public-health-service-in-midst-of-the-economic-crisis-an-opportunity-or-an-insurmountable-task

Department of Health (2001), *Quality and Fairness: A Health System for You*, Dublin: Department of Health.

HSE (2010), *HSE Monthly Performance Report*, December 2009. Dublin: HSE.

Layte, R., Nolan, A. and Nolan, B. (2007), *Poor Prescriptions, Poverty and Access to Community Health Service*, Dublin: Combat Poverty Agency.

Marmot, M. (2009), *Fair Society. Healthy Lives: The Marmot Review Full Report. Strategic Review of Health Inequalities in England post-2010*, London: UCL. Available from: http://www.ucl. ac.uk/gheg/marmotreview/FairSocietyHealthyLives

NTPF (2010), *National Treatment Purchase Fund Annual Report for 2009*, Dublin: NTPF.

OECD (2009), *Health at a Glance 2009*, OECD.

OECD (2010), *Health Institutional Characteristics: A Survey of 29 OECD Countries*, Paper No 50, OECD.

Pickett, K. and Wilkinson, R. (2009), *The Spirit Level: Why More Equal Societies Almost Always Do Better*, London: Allen Lane.

Thomas, S., Normand C. and Smith S. (2006), *Social Health Insurance in Ireland: Options for Ireland*, Dublin: The Adelaide Hospital Society / Trinity College Dublin.

Thomas, S., Normand, C. and Smith, S. (2008), *Social Health Insurance in Ireland: Further Options for Ireland*, Dublin: The Adelaide Hospital Society / Trinity College Dublin.

Thomas, S., Ryan, P. and Normand, C. (2010), *Effective Foundations for the Financing and Organisation of Social Health Insurance in Ireland*, Dublin: The Adelaide Hospital Society / Trinity College Dublin.

Tussing, A. D. and Wren, M-A., (2006), *How Ireland Cares*, Dublin: New Island.

CHAPTER FIVE

Culture and the Arts
The Possibility of An Island

Patrick Sutton

Recently I stole a teaspoon. Not just any old teaspoon from any old tea shop. No. This teaspoon is EPNS. A quality teaspoon. Not your common or garden teaspoon. Not this one. Business to Arts had arranged a meeting in the board room of the AIB Bank Centre and as we were led to the meeting we walked past works of art that most of us had only ever seen in books. We got to talking and a strange sense of ownership overcame us as we realised that the art on the walls, on the basis of the size of the bank bail out, was essentially ours and most definitely some of it was mine because when my mum died I inherited some AIB shares. Now, God forbid, we took the law into our hands and started clearing the walls. This is not Eastern Europe – we are far too middle class for that, but I did trouser a teaspoon and it sits in my study, occasionally glinting in the evening sun as a simplistic token of the savage greed of the mindless vultures who begged us all, big and small, to take out loans, regardless of our ability to pay back, to feed the beasts in the pinstripe suits who with their blinkers on screamed – profit. Huge pensions still support the shamed ones, the people who have run to the manicured hills and who wouldn't understand the word patriot if 'toirtap' was tattooed on their forehead. All has changed and there are few signs of beauty as this ship, Ireland, struggles on. The queue at airports is getting longer with people on the road again, leaving a country on its knees, a church in tatters as the pillars of society are shown up for what they are. No Skype or mobile or text message of communication will ease the broken heart of a mother who knows her daughter or son is more likely than not to be gone this time for good. This is no country for young women or men right now.

But somewhere there is a flickering light that is still stutter-

ing. As I write I am 52; I am not planning to roll up a sleeping
bag and head for Darwin. There is a spark in the fire, has to be, a
light breeze blows at the embers and it is worthwhile scratching
a little at the coals to see what is there. It is necessary to see
where the hope is. It is imperative to dust it down and see what
a future looks like. If there is no hope there is no need to go on
but we do go on and we should go on and we will go on because
of who we are, what our culture is (and has been) and how it can
best be utilised to keep us afloat. The spark, the flickering light
and the glow in the embers is the imagination. It is the one thing
that allows us to dream, to imagine, to risk and to take confident
control of who we are and what we stand for. Give a child the
framework in which she can imagine and be comfortable doing
so and that child will grow and prosper and challenge and be
challenged and have a voice that is strong, tender, articulate,
angry, beautiful and alive. This requires investment. Big investment, maybe €800 million of investment. This is the real smart
thing to do. Before any hopes are pinned on the smart economy
as the rising tide that will float all ships we need to take baby
steps first and look to the imagination to light the fuse.

The Arts Council at 70 Merrion Square is creaking with reports that tell of the value of the arts. Statistics will show the impact the arts and culture can have on people's lives. We need to
move beyond the reports and cut to the chase that is the imperative of needing to provide properly for our people. Investment in
the imagination is vital. We need to be re-turned on as a nation.
Our senses, so often numbed by the misery of bad TV, lacklustre
conversation, conditioned reactions, need to be fired up. We
need to look, listen, touch, feel and be allowed to have a response. We need to imagine, to re-imagine what we can be, we
need to become alive again as a people. We need to allow ourselves to be touched, to be articulate, to get angry and to find a
voice. We need to re-politicise ourselves through our arts and
through our culture. We need to get out of our houses and become comfortable engaging with the arts in real time. We need
to be allowed to witness beauty, we need to be allowed to cry, to
laugh and we need to be able to look at a painting or an install-
ation and know why we loathe or love it. We need to know
about aesthetics. We need to be able to figure out what it is we

stand for, our stories and songs, our photographs and our street
dancing. We need to find some kind of language that works for
us and helps us put some sense or meaning or truth onto the
chaos and beauty that is the town or city or country or world
that we live in. We need to be allowed to tell stories through our
movies and our documentaries. We need to write songs and
plays and poems and come to know that it is more than okay to
express ourselves, that indeed the act of expressing ourselves is
the very act that defines what it is we stand for as a people. We
need discourse and debate that grows from an understanding of
what we are wrestling to define. This needs to be allowed to
happen throughout the places in which we live while the walls
of the many middle class institutions need to come tumbling
down and those who wouldn't ever consider having an experience that is aesthetic in essence need to find a non-patronising
way that shares the ownership and the experience of a real
engagement with the arts and our culture.

What Ireland needs is a creative manifesto for the people.
Not a green, white or orange paper but a statement with money
and jobs and a plan attached that is a start on the road to recovery. If we can pour billions into an Anglo Irish dead black hole
and not fire up investment in the arts then the State is bankrupt
and in real trouble because the creative voice will become silent,
the imaginative response dull and the real possibility of a people
being creatively articulate in themselves will be snuffed out.

People need to experience the arts. They need to engage, to
become the artist in themselves, to realise the private touchstone
that can be the experience of hearing a song sung at a music fest-
ival that hits home, that reminds and that resonates and affirms
the whole bloody reason for living; that there are others that are
alive and on a similar road to ourselves – that we are not alone.
Dare I say that there is hope? The arts need to be something that
people do to feed themselves. Beyond the going to a gallery or
watching a play or reading a poem for the day in a Sunday
newspaper, the arts in their broadest sense need to be available
and people need to experience them because of what the reac-
tion can be. Catharsis. Affirmation. Liveness.

Finding the best way to ensure we can engage will be argued
from all sides forever. To cut to the chase, the Arts Council,

bureaucratic warts and all, needs to get more money out to more artists and arts organisations so I can engage better and challenge more and be touched more regularly. We all know that the administrators have taken over the arts. Those real statistics are, I suspect, well buried in the Merrion Square vaults. We need to trust some more that the artist we give support to is not going to piss it up against the wall. Of course there needs to be accountability but we must be flexible. Indeed I well remember the artist who got a bursary some years ago and as soon as she got the cheque went out and bought the finest leather jacket. It kept her warm, she said, and she liked how it made her feel as she set to work on doing her thing.

A couple of years ago, before the water ran out of the bath, the call to arms from the Arts Council to the government was for €100 million. In its own right and for a million good reasons, this needs to happen urgently and at once and by doing so our leaders will show their steel and show that the future has a value beyond the mere act of propping up the banks. The additional millions are being poured at everything other than the arts. I don't know why the National Campaign for the Arts have not got their way to date but perhaps if they shifted onto the streets and shouted a little louder maybe they would be better heard. The way of deciding on what money is given to which artist and what the process of accountability is needs to be radically rethought. For too long we have been guilty of inadequate decision-making. It needs to be easier to apply for money, to draw down money and to account for the money awarded. Who the experts actually are needs to be looked at and providing sufficient monies from the state will allow all the above to happen. Perhaps the Arts Council should change its name to the excellence council and play a part in helping to ensure a standard of excellence is drawn across all disciplines that raises the bar and ensures that what is supported is accessible at whatever level. If the making is private then let it be so, if it is public then let's ensure we all have a way in to it. That means spreading the message, engaging in discourse and debate, keeping ticket prices affordable and, dare I say it, providing visitors with a decent welcome and a thank you when it's all over. We need to invest in going out. Not just in the standard way but out into the world of our homes and beyond our homes with eyes open to the possibilities ... yes, the possibilities. Of what? ... of it all. The possibility of an island.

The fault line that has long been the discrepancy between what some local authorities do to define and support the arts needs to be addressed and it needs to be addressed urgently. Those with authority need to be radical and make a firm monetary commitment that by a certain date a set amount of money will be made available for a set of clearly defined arts initiatives across a local authority area. There are local authorities who still act as if the arts are some sort of annoying rash which, with a little ointment, will go away.

Beyond the Arts Council itself, where the artist is given the support of the state we need to look at how we nourish that tree. The arts without education will wither on the vine. The health of the tree won't endure. The Department of Education and Skills and the Department of Health and Children need to meet and plot and plan how they will rotavate the soil. Five central initiatives need to be defined:

One: At preschool our children need to be allowed to dream and imagine and engage in a whole range of experiences that enrich and encourage and enable the imagination to be fired up. Every child needs to be allowed to roll up their sleeves and get mucky and if that simply means more paint and more *mala* and more protective coverings and a little more time spent working with the playgroup leaders who should be trained and incentivised to encourage the imagination, then well and good. This is the important fire to light. All children need to know about story and song and imagination. Each child needs to know that play is allowed and encouraged, that fun and a little madness is alright and that laughter is contagious.

Two: Every primary school in the country needs access to a dedicated and resourced creative teacher. Someone who is trained to keep the fire alight, someone who will allow the creative idea to be followed through. This person will have undergone particular training beyond the already developing arts-based curriculum by being on call to develop the painting or drama or dance or storytelling project that is created over a period of time and shared with the wider community of the school, the village, the town, the city the region, the country, the world. The world beyond the walls of the school needs to be explored in a meaningful way above and beyond just the end of year treat to the zoo or the pantomime.

Three: Every post-primary school requires a dedicated full time staff member who has responsibility to ensure the creative soul of each individual is nurtured by leading a series of initiatives that are placed on an equal footing along with science or French to allow the often suppressed voice of post-primary students to be heard. Through writing songs and recording them, through creating plays and performing them, through the private thinking behind a poem to the battle of the bands, every young person needs to know that having a creative voice is not just the domain of the left of centre outsider but the right of all. Debate and discourse must be harnessed and each school must engage in dialogue with others beyond the school walls. The opportunity to approach arts education in a refreshing way needs to be grasped. For too long the old way has become the norm where the arts are seen as some kind of a well-meaning afterthought. To watch a young person find their voice through the poem that they write, the song that they sing or the ensemble that is created by working with others can be life affirming. Engaging our political leaders with this conversation is essential. Getting our political leaders to take a lead on this would have an impact on this country and what it can become well into the future. There is surely no greater patriotism than that.

Four: At third level and after young people have left school there need to be opportunities to engage actively in the arts as both creator and as audience. Aesthetics need to be fed into the world of the school leaver so the dream and the imagination that has been ignited at preschool, at primary and at post-primary school can further be explored not as a surprising new discovery but as a part of what makes people what they are. Beyond the drama societies and art appreciation clubs there is a need to grow opportunities that give the college student or school leaver a broad range of ways to express and explore.

Each university needs to engage a team of people who will facilitate beyond current part time *ad hoc* provision and the presidents and governing authorities and the kings and queens of the timetable need to know that engagement with the arts is as important a part of what a student might do after school or in university as anything else. To those who don't attend third level, there is a responsibility to provide community based opportunities for exploration and expression.

Five: Our experiences of the lives we lead feed our stories, and providing a network of arts practitioners to work with senior citizens will benefit not only participants but enrich society as a whole. Our old people are often overlooked and the reasonably recent arts-based initiatives for senior citizens merely go to prove how loud this particular voice can sing. Likewise in the health field, arts initiatives in hospitals, communities and the like will give expression to those who need it most.

When an individual has found themselves on a path in which the arts are a given, then and only then will a society have its eyes opened. After education, in further training and on into our working lives, we need to have had a door opened to us and to have been given the opportunity to engage and experience and respond to the art we make and the art that we see so we come to realise who we are and what we stand for as individuals and in turn as a society.

This will cost money, big money. But when you look at what money has been found to hold up our banks, it is a small and valuable investment in the heartbeat that is a nation. I suppose the important question might well be – what happens if we let the arts and culture go? What happens to us as a nation if we don't invest properly and responsibly in the arts? What do we become?

We have long valued our identity, struggled hard for it, won it with determination and with pride but it is a delicate flower and one which will become homogenised into the general field of flowers that is broadly Europe and broadly North America and broadly an identity that is not distinctive but is the same. In my view, this sameness will lead to a blandness which will lead to dulled habit and we know, from Vladimir in Beckett's *Waiting for Godot*, that 'habit is a great deadener'. I am not an economist but let me put a figure on this. €100 million for the arts council, €100 million for other cultural institutions, €100 million for preschool initiatives with €100m each to primary, post-primary, third level, community / third level initiatives and a final €100m to a National Senior Citizen arts initiative and the bill is €800 million. That's possible, surely. We should write a twenty-year Manifesto plan starting from now. We should drop a bank or two and light the fuse that is about expression and beauty and debate and discourse and anger and community and soul, song, spirit, identity and pride.

With 2016 on our doorstep – imagine an Ireland that celebrates who we are, where we come from and where we are going. If we get this right from the cradle to the grave we will have marked ourselves out, with distinction, as a great nation. It's never too late. Let's be bold and brave. Imagine an Ireland ... the possibilities of this island.

CHAPTER SIX

Population and Migration
A Vision for Social Justice

Sr Stanislaus Kennedy

The vision I have of Irish society in the next generation is one that is inclusive and respectful of all who live here. The path leading to this vision is one we must make a conscious decision to take today because the first step will require a re-examination of our views and understanding about Ireland now.

Everywhere these days there is fear, anger and distrust. Our financial system has disintegrated around us, our leaders have failed us, our church has let us down badly. Our sense of security is mortally shaken and the public mood is set on blame, scape-goating and vengeance. There is a deep and sudden rift between the people and those we see as having failed us.

There is a growing, and proper, demand for greater account-ability from our leaders, for more transparency in decision-mak-ing and for responsibility to be accepted for decisions taken. And yet, in one policy area that has transformed our country, and where mishandling or disinterest has the potential to cause deep and lasting rifts, there is little demand, and less willing-ness, for accountability, justice or open debate. That is, in rela-tion to immigration policy.

Immigration is a permanent and positive reality for Ireland. The make-up of our society has changed forever and for the bet-ter. While we were never the homogenous society that had, for many, become the accepted vision of Irish society before we became a country of net-immigration, we are now a culturally, socially and ethnically richer society.

There are undoubtedly a range of challenges that come with this change and how we respond to those challenges will have a fundamental impact on our society in the future. There remains some resistance to accepting this fundamental change and, until we overcome that resistance, we cannot take the first step on the path to ensuring we achieve a just and socially cohesive Ireland for the next generation. We betray our lack of acceptance of the diverse reality of Ireland today in our rhetoric and in our lack of action in so many areas relating to immigration and integration. The consequences of choosing the wrong path now, or choosing to stand at the crossroads unwilling to commit to action until circumstances overtake us, could prove severe.

Ireland experienced very rapid demographic change in the 1990s and in the first decade of the new millennium. On the whole, we adapted remarkably well. But we were enjoying a period of unprecedented and, unfortunately, unsustainable, growth. The economic tide has turned and, anecdotally at least, we hear of a rise in xenophobia and racism.

My vision of Ireland in the future is one where we have made a conscious and determined decision not to tolerate racism. It is one where we have accepted that we will continue to experience immigration and that its benefits are acknowledged by the community and reflected in a fair immigration system.

Ireland has all the ingredients necessary to achieve social justice and cohesion. We are compassionate, resourceful and innovative people with a commitment to justice. We can learn from the experiences, positive and negative, of other countries, adapting their lessons to our circumstances. But we must show the will to do so.

How we deal with many of the issues we face now as a result of our increased diversity – the need for clear, coherent immigration rules, how we deal with the fact that people from other countries and cultures want to identify themselves as Irish by becoming naturalised citizens, or how we will adapt the curricula of our schools to reflect our more diverse society, to name just a few examples – depends on our ability to accept and embrace the fact that the composition of our communities has changed forever, that immigration is a permanent phenomenon. That this fact has not yet been fully appreciated and accepted was particularly evident when the Irish economy began its downward spiral. Increasingly, we heard rhetoric and discourse expressing the belief that migrants would 'go home'.

The reality today is, for most people who settled here during the boom, Ireland *is* home. Accepting this reality will make us more open to addressing many of the other issues we must face as a nation. If we accept the permanent nature of immigration, then our way forward becomes a little clearer.

If we accept that Ireland will continue to be a diverse society in a generation's time, then we need to take stock of our current approach to immigration and integration laws and policies and ask if they are fit for purpose or, in fact, counterproductive.

Our approach to applications for citizenship provides a valuable insight. A migrant is eligible to apply for Irish citizenship after five years' legal residence in this country. At the moment, the government approves just over half of the applications it receives. Compare this to an approval rate of more than 90 per cent in the UK and Australia and 97 per cent in Canada. Ireland takes years to process an application for citizenship – an average of two years according to the government but, in practice, often far longer. The UK processes 95 per cent of the applications it receives within six months. Australia processes 85 per cent of its applications within 90 days. The average processing time for a citizenship application in Canada is less than a year. The length of time taken to process applications in Ireland, together with the comparatively very low approval rate, creates frustration, hurt and disillusionment amongst migrants.

One of the crucial differences between Ireland's approach to granting citizenship and that of other countries is that the Irish government tells migrants the criteria they must meet in order to apply to become a citizen, whereas other countries specify the criteria people must meet in order to be granted citizenship. In Ireland, whether or not that application is approved is completely at the discretion of the Minister for Justice and Law Reform. In other countries, Germany for example, applicants are told what criteria they must meet in order to be granted citizenship. If the criteria are met, citizenship is granted.

Many countries, including Ireland, specify that a person must be of 'good character' in order to qualify for citizenship. An applicant visiting the Australian government's website will find out what this means in practice, for example, what types of criminal offences will count against an applicant. Ireland does not spell out this criterion and it is currently interpreted as meaning that the applicant must not have come to the adverse attention of the Gardaí. So Ireland routinely rejects applications for citizenship from people who have received penalty points on their drivers' licence. Applications have been refused from people who have come to the attention of the Gardaí for issues so minor that they were not fined, did not have their drivers' licences revoked and have never been convicted of any offence. In some cases, applications have been refused without a reason being given at all.

A person whose application for naturalisation is refused has no avenue of appeal to challenge the decision.

This lack of clarity about eligibility criteria goes a long way towards explaining why the Irish government takes so long to process applications and why so many are rejected. But it also shows why there is such a strong feeling of frustration by many people who want to make a lasting commitment to this country and have been rejected.

What do we hope to achieve by refusing people citizenship on the basis that they have incurred penalty points on their driver's licence? What will it mean for Ireland in a generation's time? What does it mean for the people refused?

As mentioned above, to be eligible to apply for Irish citizenship, the applicant must have been living lawfully in Ireland for a period of five years. People who are eligible to apply are settled in Ireland and want to remain here. They are lawfully residing here and the refusal of citizenship will not, in itself, have any impact on the person's ability to continue lawfully staying in Ireland.

By refusing a citizenship application, the government is not saying the migrant must leave the country; what it is saying, however, is that the unsuccessful applicant is not fully recognised as a member of our community. The rejected applicant will not have a right to vote in national elections. They might have children who have been educated in Ireland but who will be unable to progress to third level education because, even if they performed outstandingly at school, they would be faced with the prohibitive fees applicable for non-EU citizens who study at our universities. In this situation, the children of unsuccessful applicants would also pay a penalty and would be denied the opportunity to reach their potential.

We must now make a decision about what type of society we want the next generation to enjoy. Will we, as a result of such a restrictive approach to who has the right to be considered Irish, have created a permanently segregated class of people who feel resentful and frustrated by their treatment, and with some justification? Our approach to granting citizenship risks creating a distinct class of people we will not allow to participate fully in society. Furthermore, we could be creating the circumstances where this degree of separation reaches into the next generation. What a heavy price to pay for incurring penalty points on a drivers licence!

How does Ireland benefit from this approach? And what will the impact of this approach be in terms of social cohesion in the future?

Imagine then, if we accept that our approach to granting citizenship is counterproductive and reform it. That we spell out the criteria people must meet in order to qualify for citizenship and then, if they fulfil those criteria, we grant citizenship as a right. We would have a system that takes a fraction of the time to administer because people would know if they fulfil the criteria or not. Those processing the application forms would have clear criteria to work to. There would not be the risk of generating lasting resentment among people refused citizenship for trivial reasons. Migrants who want to make a commitment to Ireland by becoming citizens would have their commitment recognised and acknowledged. Their children would not face an unnecessary hurdle in terms of reaching their full potential through access to education.

It is my hope that the next generation of Irish will reap the benefits of now reforming our current approach to granting citizenship, of making it fairer and less restrictive. This will require a significant change to current attitudes. I hope the next generation will see the value of actively encouraging migrants who have made this country home to become citizens of Ireland.

Ensuring that the next generation in Ireland enjoys social cohesion clearly requires a change in attitudes today. We can legislate to regulate behaviour, but we cannot make legislative changes to attitudes. In addition to accepting the permanently changed nature of Irish society, attitudinal change will require

leadership and education. The Irish education system has a crucial role to play.

It is my hope that, in this Ireland of the future, there will be
no difference in the educational achievements of migrant children or the children of migrants. But we must act now to ensure
that it becomes a reality.

We can learn from countries with more experience as 'countries of destination', like Canada and Australia. In Canada and
Australia, educational disadvantage experienced by migrants
has evened out by the second generation. What are those countries doing better than those countries where migrant children
and the children of migrants perform less well at school? Can
we learn from their experience and implement changes to our
approach to education in Ireland?

Is our curriculum reflective of our cultural diversity? It is
crucial that our education system reflects society's diversity. For
that reason, it is time now for the church to consider and to plan
for the withdrawal from running schools in Ireland and focus
instead on ensuring faith is transferred. It is the State's job to
plan for the education needs of our diverse population. The
church's role is very different. Its task is to spread the faith,
ethos and values of the church, but also to acknowledge the
ethos and values of other religions and faiths.

Can we learn from Canada and Australia, and other countries
who have a strong commitment to language tuition? Are we prepared to invest in the provision of English language tuition for
migrants in Ireland? What cost will we bear if we don't? Again,
if we accept that immigration is a permanent reality, then this
question becomes easier to answer. We must make this investment now. We know that the risks of not investing in language
tuition can be ghettoisation, lack of integration, economic and
educational disadvantage. If we accept that our communities
have changed forever and we don't want to create the circumstances just described, then the path we must choose is clear.

Let's now imagine a child born into the new, ideal, socially
just Ireland. It might be born into a struggling inner-city family
or into a middle-class suburban family, into an immigrant family
or a Traveller family; it might be a girl or a boy; it might be born
into a two-parent family or the child of a single mother; it might

be a healthy child, or a child born with HIV or with a disability; it might be a little Muslim or a little Catholic or the child of secular parents; its mother-tongue might be English or Irish, Polish or French or Arabic.

Whatever its family background, genetic heritage, cultural identity or health status, it is easy to recognise and natural to want to respond to the vulnerability and myriad needs of a new baby. Nor is it hard to extend this thinking and to agree that all our children should be able to grow up free of violence, oppression, discrimination, abuse and addiction, to be safe from trafficking, slavery and exploitation, and to have their health, housing, educational and economic needs met, as of right.

When the time comes for our imagined child to go to preschool and later to primary school, he or she needs to have a place that is suitable for his or her needs, preferably at a local school that is adequately resourced to meet the needs of all the community's children, including those with physical or intellectual disabilities, psychological or emotional problems or learning difficulties and, especially in the case of migrant children, language needs.

In order to meet the needs of all the children they serve, schools need to be properly resourced by the State. Education is highly valued in our society, but it is often thought of as an economic rather than a social and a moral good, and it is sad to hear debates about educational resources being reduced to a discussion about whether or not a particular pupil-teacher ratio is consistent with economic achievement. In a future socially just Ireland, education would be valued for its own sake as well as for the economic benefits that it can bring to society and the individual.

As our imaginary child emerges from adolescence and starts to think about taking his or her place in the adult world, their needs will change again. The young person needs the kind of route into adult life that best suits his or her talents and abilities, whether that is a place in a college or university or an appropriate job. If the child of a migrant does well at school in Ireland, the immigration status of his or her parents should not effectively prevent them from studying at third level through the charging of fees that apply to non-EU citizens.

Not everyone can have a job that is glamorous and thrilling, but everyone needs a job, and everyone's workplace should be a place where they are respected and where they can respect themselves as contributing to society, where they can earn a decent living wage and where their talents and skills are valued. In a socially just Ireland, equal opportunities and anti-discrimination legislation would effectively uphold the rights of everyone in the workplace and in the community more generally.

Adults' needs also change over time, and at some point everyone needs to avail of services such as housing, continuing education and medical or psychiatric treatment, counselling and support in the face of difficulties such as bereavement, addiction, mental illness, financial difficulty or family breakdown, so that the person is constantly supported to live the best life they can as far as possible as part of a community and in the company of family and friends. Accessing these services would not preclude anyone from being granted citizenship in a socially just future Ireland.

All people living in Ireland should also have access to sports and the arts, as participants or spectators, to community and civic life and to social discourse, public debate and political participation.

As middle age settles on our imaginary resident in the new, socially just Ireland, he or she should be enabled and supported to look after his or her dependants, who may now be older family members rather than children, and to plan for his or her own retirement and old age. A socially just society would allow him or her to age at their own pace, including allowing older people to work for as long as they are able and willing to work, with the option to withdraw gradually from the workplace, as their circumstances change.

A society built on social justice and responsive to the needs of the people living within its borders would provide a variety of options for older people and a continuum of care, depending on the person's developing needs. Elderly people should be supported to live independently for as long as that is their wish, with appropriate household help or nursing or medical services as necessary; with easy access to sheltered or supportive housing as they become more dependent, and access also to hospital and nursing care if they become ill or frail and are no longer able to care for themselves.

If we can agree that every child born into our society deserves what it needs, in childhood, youth, adulthood, middle age and old age, then we are signing up to the idea of social justice, because that is in essence what social justice is about: it is about meeting everyone's needs as a right, providing for everyone not according to their income level or their social status, their gender or their skin colour or their cultural identity, but according to their needs and circumstances.

We have a golden opportunity now, when the values of the marketplace are so clearly in disgrace and we are demanding more accountability and responsibility from our leaders, to rethink our whole approach to society and to accept and implement not just change but what amounts to social revolution. But social revolution doesn't happen on the streets – it happens in hearts and minds, and it has to be thought through and planned for. Planning has never been our strong point as a people, partly because our political system lends itself to short-term thinking; but we have to learn now to think ahead, and to overhaul the infrastructures of our society and put in place infrastructures that will support social justice.

Most of all we need to accept that our communities have changed forever. They are more culturally diverse and the richer for it. If we want to ensure that future generations living in Ireland enjoy socially cohesive communities, then we have an obligation to act now. What is needed in this country now, more than ever, is informed debate about immigration and inclusion, backed by legislation and policies which are clear, fair and transparent.

CHAPTER SEVEN

Education
Education for the 21st century – a new paradigm

Prof Tom Collins/Rose Dolan

There are two separate languages now – the language of economics and the language of ecology, and they do not converge. The language of economics is attractive, and remains so, because it is politically appealing. It offers promises. It is precise, authoritative, aesthetically pleasing. Policy-makers apply the models, and if they don't work there is a tendency to conclude that it is reality that is playing tricks. The assumption is not that the models are wrong but that they must be applied with greater rigour ... While the many deficiencies and limitations of the theory that support the old paradigm must be overcome (mechanistic interpretations and inadequate indicators of well-being, among others), a theoretical body for the new paradigm must still be constructed. (Manfred Max-Neef)

The literature on disasters draws attention to a number of common features which all disasters typically share. These include the fact that most disasters are either based on human failure or miscalculation, or their worst consequences are derived from this rather than from natural phenomena or even technological failure. Even disasters such as earthquakes, which are of course natural phenomena, have effects which are greatly mitigated or exacerbated by the effectiveness of the human dimension as in the quality of building and construction work or the effectiveness of emergency services.

Secondly many disasters are preceded by generalised overconfidence. The current economic crisis in Ireland, for instance, was preceded by the exuberance of the Celtic Tiger. The sinking of the *Titanic* followed a widely held view that it was an unsinkable ship. The fall of Troy was precipitated by the rulers of Troy themselves bringing the Trojan Horse inside the unbreachable walls.

Such overconfidence is often accompanied by a refusal to read the signals. It is said for instance that the *Titanic* received numerous ice warnings on the day it hit the glacier. The current problems with banking in Ireland are a result of the failure of bank regulations in Celtic Tiger Ireland. At an individual level, many chronic illnesses arise from a failure to read signals or address symptoms early enough.

Overconfidence also results in a puerile belief in one's own immortality and in ignoring the precautions that one would prudently take in the event of one's expectations not being realised. Again for instance in the case of the *Titanic*, there were enough lifeboats to meet the needs of only half the passengers.

Finally many disasters are characterised by a poor adaptation to the crisis or even a denial that any crisis is occurring. In much the same way as Nero fiddled while Rome burned, the band continued to play on the upper decks of the *Titanic* as the ship was submerged at the lower levels. More recently, bankers throughout the world continued to pay themselves substantial bonuses as the foundations of their enterprises collapsed and as their parent States had to take on the task of rescuing them.

The climate change crisis and the world response to it share many of these features. Even as there is an ever growing acceptance in the public consciousness of the impending crisis of global warming, a minority deny it and the majority ignore it.

Within a context of generalised failure to craft meaningful and profound institutional responses to global warming, that of education is of particular concern. This arises from a number of factors arguably the most potent of which is that formalised education is itself a product of the industrial age and persists with structures, processes and mindsets which have their roots in this epoch and which are singularly unsuited to the challenges of a post-industrial era in which the environmental crisis looms ever larger.

This failure is partly due to the social origins of formalised education and its emergence as a direct response to the needs created by the industrial revolution. In The New Industrial State,[1] the economist John Kenneth Galbraith held that mass literacy –

---

1. Galbraith (1967)

the defining contribution of universal education – resulted less from a widely held concern for public enlightenment and rather more from a concern to meet the needs of an industrial economy. Indeed he went on to suggest that if the need of the economy was for 'millions of unlettered proletarians', this very likely is what the education system would have delivered.

But it was not only in its message through which schooling addressed the needs of industry, it was also in its medium. Toffler[2] calls attention to the ways in which the structures, processes and culture of schools replicate those of the factory. He saw the factory as the defining institution of the industrial era, underpinned by what he referred to as a code which consisted of six universal principles. These principles of standardisation, synchronisation, concentration, specialisation, maximisation and centralisation became the blueprint for many of the institutional creations of the industrial era, including the school. The school replicated the assembly line in the manner of its organisation, the reliance on specialists, the reductionist mechanistic approach to the organisation of knowledge in breaking it into its component parts (subjects) and attempting to reassemble it, in the tight attention to rigid timetables wherein large groups of similarly aged people are managed to very high levels of precision and in the reliance on formalised managers and managerial processes in highly organised bureaucracies for its organisational coherence. Even in layout and design, the school would come to incorporate many of the features associated with industrial age buildings such as factories, hospitals or railway stations.

Within this perspective, students of course come to be seen simply as raw material to which value is added by a process which they undergo and after which they are subjected to standard assessment/examination processes to establish if indeed this value added process has been successful. The work of Postman and Weingartner draws attention to the 'hidden curriculum' of schooling with the focus on rote learning and submissive behaviour as key requirements for the boring repetitive mindlessness of assembly line work. The 'hidden curriculum' unfolds in the following ways:

2. Toffler (1980)

- Knowledge is beyond the power of students and is in any case, none of their business.
- Recall is the highest form of intellectual achievement – the collection of 'facts' is the goal of education.
- The voice of authority is to be trusted more than independent judgement.
- One's own ideas and those of classmates are inconsequential.
- Feelings are irrelevant in education.
- There is always a single unambiguous answer to any question.
- Passive acceptance is a more desirable response to ideas than active criticism.[3]

Bowles and Gintis[4] developed the concept of the 'hidden curriculum' by advancing the position that schools accomplish this goal by what they call the 'correspondence principle', i.e. by structuring social interactions and individual rewards to replicate the environment of the workplace. This view is supported by Leighton in relation to education in England, where 'pupils are still largely expected to be passive recipients of learning about their place in society'.[5]

There is now a growing body of evidence that this model of schooling is no longer fit for purpose on many levels and that the tensions arising from such misalignment are becoming ever more apparent. Recent work in Ireland by the ESRI and the NCCA[6] involving a longitudinal study of 900 second level students throughout their secondary schooling, draws attention to the high levels of disengagement amongst students, significant problems of stress and mental health, boredom, a reliance on didactic pedagogical approaches, particularly in examination classes together with an over-reliance on memorisation and rote learning, and the close relationship between the child's socio-economic background and educational outcomes.[7] However,

---

3. Postman and Weingartner (1969), pp. 20-21
4. Bowles and Gintis (1976)
5. Leighton (2006), p. 80
6. See Smyth *et al* (2004), Smyth *et al* (2006) and Smyth *et al* (2007)
7. Details of this research are available at http://www.ncca.ie/en/ Curriculum_and_Assessment/Post-Primary_ Education/ Junior_Cycle/ Research_on_students%27_experiences

the concern with schooling is not confined to those with a direct engagement with it. Third level institutions and employers consistently point to the inappropriateness of this approach to learning for success in higher education and in the modern workplace. They call repeatedly for learners who are self-directed and self-motivated; who are solution oriented, can work in teams and can formulate innovative and creative approaches to solving problems.

In view of these challenges, there is an ever more persuasive argument for rethinking education. It is important that any such revisitation be driven by considerations that are primarily to do with human and social development, and less to do with economic or any other extraneous or instrumental consideration. In particular, however, it must be driven by the realisation that the context in which schooling emerged has been profoundly altered and that this new context must underpin the structure and purpose of the school of the future. It is to this fundamental rethinking challenge which Bateson refers when she notes that

> Our machines, our value systems, our educational systems will all have to be informed by (the) switch, from the machine age when we tried to design schools to be like factories, to an ecological age, when we want to design schools, families and social institutions in terms of maintaining the quality of life, not just for our species, but for the whole planet.[8]

Connectedness and Depletion

One of the ironies of the cyber age is a growing conviction that young people who are actively involved and engaged in the computing cloud of mass information and networking are also profoundly disconnected socially and even intrapersonally in terms of their own mental health. The sociological question which this presents is one which wonders about the possibility of being connected globally but being disconnected locally. Is it possible therefore that the socialisation of the child which formerly relied on intimate face to face relationships as the primary if not the complete source of socialisation can now move to a cyber community, replacing these locally based intimate connections?

8. Bateson (1997), p 84

It is possible to contend that as biodiversity diminishes in the biological world, it is also diminishing in the social world of the child, providing a depleted emotional and psychological context in a sea of information. Multiple learning or developmental zones and sites have disappeared from the social world of the child much as they have in the ecosphere. These include the spontaneous and unplanned for learning which the child acquired in the day to day activities of unsupervised play, of exploring the neighbourhood, of encountering a range of people who had a distinct meaning to him or her, of becoming familiar with the landscape – historical, social and physical – and of gradually learning to navigate a local world. To the extent that place may be defined as space with meaning, the child acquired his or her sense of self and identity within the richness of an environment that had a capacity to nurture learning and the holistic development of the child.

There is a growing body of literature on the theme of well-being and on the challenges to well-being of contemporary childhood. According to Sue Palmer, 'every year children become more distractible, impulsive and self-obsessed – less able to learn, to enjoy life, to thrive socially'.[9] While Palmer attributes much of the ennui of childhood to the proliferation of electronic media and to the time children spend on such media, it is likely to have a deeper source. This lies in the definition of children as consumers and, as a consequence, the denial of their capacity to create their own world and their own well-being.

In the 1970s the philosopher Erich Fromm distinguished between a state of having and a state of being. He considered that in a consumerist world, the pursuit of happiness through material abundance and the domination of nature would prove illusory. He argued instead that human fulfilment lay not in the promise of materialist accumulation but in a greater awareness of the needs of the individual's inner self. Spiritual development, as Fromm saw it, was the ultimate goal and this would be blunted or pre-empted by a preoccupation with consumption and acquisitiveness.

If one considers the nature of childhood in contemporary

9. Palmer (2006)

society from this perspective, it could be argued that childhood has become a stage of consumption rather than a stage of creation. In this way, the underpinning foundations of a healthy and developmental childhood are weakened. Children in modern Ireland, for instance, spend on average 18 hours per week looking at television. It is useful to consider what childhood activities have been displaced by this activity over the last 40 years and if these activities, whatever their nature, had greater or lesser developmental value than looking at television?

A view of childhood well-being as a consequence of creative activity is consistent with Toffler's concept of the 'prosumer'. For Toffler, the defining feature of the industrial era is the 'invisible wedge' of the marketplace. As he presents it, the marketplace emerged during the industrial era as the first occasion in human history where the producer and the consumer were no longer connected in some personal way. Furthermore, as production systems evolved in factories, producers increasingly found themselves producing components of the finished product rather than the finished product itself. In this way the producers became disconnected simultaneously from their products and from those who were using their products.

Toffler suggests that in a post-industrial 'third wave' society, it will be necessary to re-establish the connection between production and consumption, hence his concept of the 'prosumer'. This concept is sometimes represented as mass customisation i.e. the tailoring of consumer products to individual specifications. This, however, is to see the concept as merely a further refinement of mass consumption rather than one of re-establishing the spiritual connection between the production and the consumption of goods.

This disconnect between production and consumption enables the unlimited exploitation of resources because the consumer is rarely challenged with the consequences of their consumption. This allows for practices of food production which involve the intensive rearing of animals, an excessive reliance on chemical interventions such as pesticides and insecticides, and the possibility of the genetic modification of animals and plants.

A view of the child as a prosumer would aim to reconnect and revalue the processes of production with consumption and would recognise the multiple learning and developmental dimensions to which such a reconnection would give rise. The child, for instance, who bakes a cake with a parent will enter the world of ratios in calculating the proportions of the different ingredients, will be introduced to weights and measures, will learn about the origin and composition of different ingredients, will understand temperature, will develop negotiating, listening and teamwork skills as the baking process unfolds, will share in the ritual and ceremony of taking the cake from the oven and of sharing it with family members and will build a mental association between the concept of endeavour and that of pleasure. Whether the cake is a success or a failure, the learning is advanced. All of these opportunities are lost where the cake is only ever acquired from a supermarket shelf.

School as a Prosuming Zone
As we enter the second decade of the 21st century, we have arrived at a point in history where the obsessive pursuit of consumerism has resulted in the depletion of the earth's resources, a build up of toxic waste in the environment and the weakening of human capability. Human civilisation is now presented with the challenge of reversing these processes and of discovering and adopting a more sustainable trajectory.

The work of Karl-Henrik Robèrt is instructive here. In his formulation of The Natural Step,[10] he addresses a concern that the drive to sustainability be underpinned by sound scientific analysis in the first instance and by generalised global agreement around what he terms the four principles of sustainability. These may be represented as opposite.[11]

He has built a planning framework on these four principles which he terms the Framework for Sustainable Strategic Development (FSSD). The framework is book ended around an agreement on the 'shape of success'. This agreement can apply either at an individual level or at any organisational level. Crucially the shape of success has to be circumscribed by the tolerance level of the system in which it is operating. He argues that the earth's system has differential tolerance levels for toxic

10. Robèrt (2002)
11. Adapted from http://www.naturalstep.org/the-system-conditions.

In a sustainable society, nature is not subject to systematically increasing:	To become a sustainable society we must:
1. concentrations of substances extracted from the earth's crust.	1. eliminate our contribution to the progressive build up of substances extracted from the Earth's crust (for example, heavy metals and fossil fuels).
2. concentrations of substances produced by society.	2. eliminate our contribution to the progressive build up of chemicals and compounds produced by society.
3. degradation by physical means.	3. eliminate our contribution to the progressive physical degradation and destruction of nature and natural processes (for example, excessive harvesting of forests and encroaching on or eliminating critical wildlife habitat).
4. and, in that society, people are not subject to conditions that systemically undermine their capacity to meet their needs.	4. eliminate our contribution to conditions that undermine people's capacity to meet their basic human needs (for example, unsafe working conditions and not enough pay to live on).

substances and that all decision-making at both private and corporate level should be informed by such considerations.

Having agreed the shape of success and identified the system tolerance levels, he advocates a process which he refers to as 'backcasting' i.e. in imagining that this success has already been arrived at, one then describes the policies and practices that connect the future with the present.[12]

If we approach the issue of education and schooling from the perspective of The Natural Step, we ask what is the shape of a successful education system in the future, bearing in mind the challenges to it outlined earlier in the chapter. If the shape of success involves effectively addressing the current shortcomings, it

12. Holmberg and Robèrt (2000), pp 291-308

might be argued that a successful education system is one where the system is realigned to meet both the needs of the child and the needs of the world. This would presuppose an education system in which

- The child encounters his or her own potential for self creation and agency.
- The child develops an awareness of the relationship between individual actions and social and ecological impact.
- The child experiences a curriculum which focuses on the vulnerability of the earth's systems and that the knowledge, attitudes and skills acquired in the school would be derived from an assumption of this vulnerability.
- The child develops a capacity to interrogate his or her learning and moral position in terms of his or her responsibility to the collective.
- The child learns to live with difference as an enriching dimension of life.
- The child learns that every one, regardless of individual ability or disability, can contribute to communal well-being.

A focus on sustainable education would be preoccupied with ensuring that students acquired a capacity for self-generation and self-renewal through their life course and that in their impact on the world, they would also enhance its capacity for self-generation and renewal. It would therefore revisit the intellectual content of education as to its capacity to generate or heal rather than deplete. It would build on interdisciplinary connections between formerly segregated subject areas and ensure that students acquire the capacity to subject all decision-making to a transparent process of ethical interrogation, itself circumscribed by the question of the system's tolerance capacity.

It echoes Sterling's definition of sustainable education as:

a change of educational culture, one which develops and embodies the theory and practice of sustainability in a way which is critically aware. It is therefore a transformative paradigm which values, sustains and realises human potential in relation to the need to attain and sustain social, economic and ecological well-being, recognising that they must be part of the same dynamic.[13]

13. Sterling (2001), p 22

The changes indicated here imply a profound systemic and paradigmatic shift in every aspect of educational provision, moving it from being an agent of the industrial production system to one of reconstruction, regeneration and reconnection. A view of education as an ethical and moral project as opposed to a merely utilitarian or instrumental service to economic interests is consistent with this goal of reconnection.

It is likely that this change can only happen on the back of a recognition that we are in a period of intense and urgent planetary crisis and that we can no longer refuse to read the signals of an impending and inevitable disaster.

References:

Bateson, M. C. (1997), 'Understanding Natural Systems', in C. Zelov and P. Cousineau, *Design Outlaws on the Ecological Frontier*, Philadelphia: Knossus Publishing.

Bowles, S. and Gintis, H. (1976), *Schooling in Capitalist America*, London: Routledge.

Fromm, E. (1976), *To Have or to Be*, London: Continuum.

Galbraith, J. K. (1967), *The New Industrial State*, Boston: Houghton Mifflin.

Holmberg, J. and Robèrt, K-H. (2000), Backcasting from non-overlapping sustainability principles – a framework for strategic planning, *International Journal of Sustainable Development and World Ecology 7*.

Leighton, R. (2006), Revisiting Postman and Weingartner's 'New Education' – is Teaching Citizenship a Subversive Activity? *Citizenship and Teacher Education*, 2 (1).

Max-Neef, M., retrieved from http://www.rightlivelihood.org/max-neef.pdf

Palmer, S. (2006), *Toxic Childhood: How the Modern World is damaging our children and what we can do about it*, London: Orion.

Postman, N. and Weingartner, C. (1969), *Teaching as a Subversive Activity*, London: Penguin.

Robèrt, K-H. (2002), *The Natural Step Story: Seeding a Quiet Revolution*, Gabriola Island, BC: New Society Publishers.

Smyth, E., Dunne, A., McCoy, S. and Darmody, M, (2006), *Pathways through the junior cycle: The experiences of second year students*, Dublin: The Liffey Press in association with the Economic and Social Research Institute.

Smyth, E., Dunne, A., Darmody, M. and McCoy, S. (2007), *Gearing Up for the Exam? The Experiences of Junior Certificate Students*, Dublin: The Liffey Press in association with The Economic and Social Research Institute.

Smyth, E., McCoy, S. and Darmody, M. (2004), *Moving Up: The experiences of first year students in post-primary education*, Dublin: The Liffey Press in association with the Economic and Social Research Institute.

Sterling, S. (2001), *Sustainable Education – Re-Visioning Learning and Change*, Schumacher Society, Briefing no 6, Dartington: Green Books.

Toffler, A. (1980), *The Third Wave*, London: Collins.

CHAPTER EIGHT

Innovation and Enterprise
Creating an Ecosystem for Social Innovation

Paul O'Hara

As a medical student during the 1980s, Steve Collins spent his summer holidays backpacking across Africa – a less worn track for European students. When he arrived in a famished Sudan, he realised he couldn't be a tourist amongst such suffering and helped out as he could. Returning to Africa as a doctor throughout the 1990s to work in various famines, Steve could see the models for treating malnutrition were ineffective. He created two new organisations for the treatment and prevention of malnutrition including Valid International, to develop new community-based distribution models, and Valid Nutrition to produce therapeutic foods. Steve's model significantly reduces fatalities from acute malnutrition, has been endorsed by the UN and World Health Organisation as best practice, and has been adopted in over thirty countries. Steve is a social entrepreneur, living in West Cork, whose innovations have changed the world.

If Ireland is to survive the mounting social and environmental challenges and thrive in an increasingly competitive global economy, we must focus as a nation on multiplying the number of innovators – this is our most critical opportunity. The key factor for the success of any human grouping, be it a company, city or country will be the proportion of its people that are innovators.

The organisations, cities and countries fostering and attracting innovative talent are those that give people the time and resources to explore their potential and passion, regardless of position. Google and Silicon Valley are exemplars in creating a culture where everyone can be a changemaker. Nations and organisations that run command and control structures are dying away. Who wants to be a passive participant when they could be changemakers, when they could live lives far more creative and contributory and therefore respected and valued?

Imagine an Ireland where every individual has the confidence and skills to create and execute solutions for social, economic or environmental problems wherever they might exist. Evidenced by our mounting economic, social and environmental challenges, and our loss of competitiveness in the global economy, Ireland is not transitioning quickly enough to a society where everyone innovates. Changemakers are the catalysts for converting the challenges we face into opportunities.

The 'big five' challenges of climate change, unemployment, marginalisation, an ageing population and unsustainable public finances threaten to sink Ireland and will require nothing less than radical and large scale innovation over the short, medium and long term. Each challenge is both local and international in scope and each represents enormous opportunity for innovation, meaningful job creation and growth. The focus of innovation and R&D investment should be focused on pursuing these large international opportunities, offering tremendous leverage on all resources. Let's focus our talents and resources on building sustainable economic growth, sustainable public finances and sustainable use of natural resources while ending marginalisation and unemployment. This must be the role of the innovation society.

Rather than focus on the specific challenges, let us focus on the innovation opportunity and the kind of society we need to harness it. A 'knowledge' or 'smart' economy is meaningless – unless harnessed productively for the benefit of all. What is certainly needed is an 'innovation' society that will unleash the creative and entrepreneurial potential of all people to create and execute real solutions for real needs. This chapter focuses on how we can multiply the number of innovators in society and some of the blocks needed to build an ecosystem for social innovation to flourish.

Innovation is a process distinct from 'improvement' or 'change' and from 'creativity' and 'invention'. Creativity and invention are central to the innovation process but overlook the critical stages of implementation and diffusion which make new ideas useful. Though most commonly associated with business, innovation exists in every field of human endeavour from the arts to education to economic development and across the boundaries of every sector including the business, public and citizen sectors. Innovations are almost always driven by entrepreneurial individuals and teams from within or outside organisations.

Social innovations are distinct in that they have the aim of meeting society's needs. Social innovations span everything from Montessori schools to Wikipedia, restorative justice to community policing, micro finance to fair trade, person centred social services to hotlines for older people, citizen journalism to green schools, community wind farms to carbon trading, to name just a few areas.

Behind each of these social innovations, there is a social entrepreneur or social intrapreneur. A powerful example of a social entrepreneur in Ireland is Sister Stanislaus Kennedy who founded Focus Ireland, The Immigrant Council of Ireland, Social Innovations Ireland and co-founded Young Social Innovators. Social entrepreneurs are not content to give a fish or teach how to fish; they will not rest until they have revolutionised the entire fishing industry.

Social entrepreneurs change systems in several different ways:

- Redefining interconnections in market systems (market dynamics and value chains);
- Changing the rules that govern our societies (public policy and industry norms);
- Transforming the meaning of private *vs* citizen sector (business social congruence);
- Fully integrating marginalised populations (full citizenship and empathetic ethics);
- Increasing the number of people who are social problem solvers (culture of changemaking and social entrepreneurship).

The infrastructure of supports for private sector innovation is relatively well established in Ireland and the recent report by the government appointed Innovation Taskforce outlines valuable next steps. However, the infrastructure for social innovation is non-existent by comparison. To foster social innovation in Ireland, we need to develop an ecosystem of supports, borrowing from and building upon those developed for the private sector. At the core of this ecosystem are social entrepreneurs/ intrapreneurs and their organisations, both Irish and international. Additional elements of the ecosystem include: the education system; grant, debt and equity finance; public policy; public and private institutions; and investment in research and development.

The following principals must underpin such an ecosystem:

- The social entrepreneurs/intrapreneurs and their organisations must be at the centre of all efforts;
- Cultivating, growing and attracting social entrepreneurs and their organisations;
- The availability of grant, debt and/or equity finance at the development, launch and growth stages is critical;
- An education system which fosters empathy, creativity, resourcefulness, teamwork and leadership is essential to building an innovation society;
- The State must recognise the value of social innovation, showcase role models and invest in its development.

What do we need to do to make this happen?
Education should be about equipping young people with the knowledge, tools and skills they need to achieve their full potential. There is much that is good about the Irish education system including many brilliant and passionate teachers. Yet, against this metric of putting people on track to achieve their full potential, we fail miserably. Being a top performing student academically is no indicator for success. First of all, how many young people end up doing what they are most passionate about – a key factor for success? Too many are doing things that make them miserable which is an unacceptable waste of human capacity. Secondly, too many graduates are ill-equipped for a rapidly changing world that demands the critical skills of empathy, creativity, resourcefulness, teamwork and leadership. However, writing these words into a curriculum is completely inadequate. These are skills that can only be developed through experiential learning. The pace of change outside the school walls is far outstripping that within and we utterly fail every young person as a result, either in ignorance, complicity or some combination of both. There are few comparable injustices. We must rethink and

redesign the education system at all levels to equip every young person with what they need to achieve their full potential and find their true passion. The learned skills of empathy, creativity, resourcefulness, teamwork and leadership are central skills for building an innovation society where everyone can be a change-maker.

Empathy is the ability to share another being's feelings and emotions and respond accordingly. Some psychologists describe evil as the absence of empathy. The opposite is certainly true. In her capacity as President of Ireland, Mary Robinson visited Somalia after the crisis there in 1992. She describes her unpreparedness for the scale of human suffering – the lines of women and men with starving children. In a media address during the visit, a visibly emotional Mary said, 'I have such a sense of what the world must take responsibility for. And by the world, I don't mean some distant sources, I mean each of us.' Mary not only felt the suffering of the people she met in Somalia, she has committed her life to campaigning tirelessly and selflessly on behalf of those that suffer the shameful injustices of poverty and oppression. This is a perfect example of the power of applied empathy, a most powerful force for good.

Where empathy exists, the exposure to suffering demands a compassionate response. Thankfully, many Irish people have the capacity to empathise. Regrettably, too few have developed the creativity, resourcefulness and leadership capacity to respond with the power and compassion and impact they have the capacity for. Not only is this a huge loss for society, but it can also be incredibly debilitating for the individual. Mary Robinson has now shifted her focused efforts to shining a light on the injustices of climate change – humanity's existential challenge. Responding to this daunting challenge will require, among other things, an empathetic revolution.

So what can we do to foster empathy in young people across Ireland? *Roots of Empathy* is an evidence-based classroom programme whose mission is to build peaceful and civil societies – child by child – through the development of empathy in children. The programme was founded in Canada in 1996 by social entrepreneur Mary Gordon, and today has reached more than 315,000 children worldwide. At the heart of the programme are

classroom visits by an infant and parent. Through guided observations of this loving relationship, children learn to identify and
reflect on their own thoughts and feelings and those of others
(empathy). Independent evaluations consistently show children
who participate in *Roots of Empathy* experience dramatic and
lasting effects in terms of increased pro-social behavior (sharing,
helping and including) and decreased aggression. *Roots of
Empathy* has been recognised by the Dalai Lama, Daniel
Goleman – author of *Emotional Intelligence*, Jeremy Rifkin – author of *The Empathetic Civilization*, the World Health Organisation and UN among others. *Roots of Empathy* starts in forty primary schools across the island of Ireland during 2010.

Creativity is central to the innovation process – in the creation
of new ideas that have value, in problem solving and in vision
setting. How can we even contemplate an innovation society
without actively fostering a creative people? Sir Ken Robinson,
who is both expert and compelling on this topic, believes the
education system as currently designed is ruthlessly killing the
potential of children. Quoting from his now famous TED[1] lec-
ture in 2006, 'Children are not afraid of being wrong. What we
know is that if you're not prepared to be wrong, you will never
come up with anything original. By the time they get to be
adults, most kids have lost that capacity – they have become
frightened of being wrong. We run our companies like this – we
stigmatise mistakes, and we're now running national education
systems where mistakes are the worst thing you can make and
the result is that we are educating people out of their creative
capacities. Picasso once said that all children are born artists, the
problem is to remain an artist as we grow up. We don't grow
into creativity, we grow out of it, or rather, we get educated out
of it.'

Creativity is important in all endeavours, not just in the arts
with which it is most closely associated. There are certainly
many powerful examples of creative people throughout Irish
history and many living today. And yet, we have a culture in
Irish society that stigmatises mistakes, dampening the very
thing that drives us forward. In such a culture, creativity neces-

---

1. Technology, Entertainment, Design. A non-profit organisation devoted
to Ideas Worth Spreading.

sitates extraordinary courage. This culture has its roots in our education system.

We must, starting with the education system, provide the ideal conditions for people and their ideas to grow, where people bring and do their best. You can't make people develop, you can't make them grow, you can't make them creative, you can't make them find their talent – any more than a farmer makes his crop grow. A farmer understands the right conditions in which a crop will grow. Like the farmer, we must understand the optimum conditions for growth in our people. Let us invite Ken Robinson to co-create these conditions with us.

The innovation process requires more than creativity. Almost everyone has an idea to change the world, but too few have the confidence and skills to make them a reality – a shocking waste of human ingenuity. It requires leadership and resourcefulness to make an idea a reality – both learned skills. Leadership is the ability to bring others on a journey towards a shared vision while creating an environment for everyone to contribute – the ability to create mass collaboration around a particular idea. It is very difficult to teach leadership in a classroom, but much easier to create opportunities for people to experience it and learn how to do it – that is what builds both capability and confidence. Ask any leading entrepreneur when they had their first entrepreneurial experience and they will likely trace back to their teenage years and sometimes even earlier. This early years experience is essential to building the confidence and skills required for an innovation society. There are large numbers of 'highly qualified' young people in Ireland unemployed today. While we challenge them to take a risk and start their own business, the reality is that most are completely ill equipped to do so and will have to leave Ireland to find employment.

Think of all the reasons we offer when we failed to achieve something: 'didn't have the money, the time, the knowledge, the team, the experience or the contacts' and so on. These may well be true, but they are excuses. Far too often, the underlying reason for not achieving something is that we lacked the resourcefulness. We lacked the creativity, the determination, the passion or the authentic motivation to get it done. This lack of resourcefulness is what smothers so many dreams and keeps so many ideas as unrealised aspirations. There are several ways to develop these skills in young people, from team sports to programmes that facilitate venture start-ups such as Youth Venture.

Youth Venture was created by Bill Drayton, the founder and CEO of Ashoka, to address these very challenges. Youth Venture gives young people across the world the challenge, the tools and the space to dream up an idea to change their community, and then the financial and practical supports to work in teams to make those ideas a reality and grow them. The young people get to experience the entire innovation process, starting radio stations, magazines, bike repair shops, and tutorial groups. Taking an idea from creative thought to executed reality gives young people the confidence and skills to do it over and over throughout life, building ambition and impact as belief and ability grows. Social philosopher Charles Handy describes this process as 'planting the golden seed'. To believe in someone is one of the greatest gifts. A society where everyone can be a changemaker is an unreachable fantasy unless the youth years become years of practising being powerful and acquiring the required underlying skills.

There are several examples of organisations in Ireland fostering these entrepreneurial skills in young people through schools including Young Social Innovators, co-founded by Rachel Collier and Sister Stanislaus Kennedy, Jerry Kennelly's Young Entrepreneur Programme in Kerry, the National Foundation for Teaching Entrepreneurship which is run in Ireland by Foróige, the BT Young Scientist Awards and the County Enterprise Boards Student Enterprise Awards. It is essential that every young person, during their teenage years, gain the experience of coming up with an idea and executing it if we are to build an innovation society. This is an absolutely critical and undervalued insight in Ireland.

Bill Gates recently completed a university tour in the United States. His purpose was to challenge the best and brightest to work on the world's greatest challenges. He discovered a growing interest and momentum. There is overwhelming evidence that people want meaningful work. The assumption that human beings are driven by profit alone is outdated. Need for achievement remains, but more and more people choose to do good while doing well. The organisations, regardless of sector, that work towards a bigger ideal than profit, are increasingly attracting the best talent. This is an irreversible trend. This is where the job growth is, not to mention the most challenging, value-rooted and increasingly well paid jobs. Across the world, the citizen sector is generating jobs three times as fast as business. Every major business school in the western world has growing numbers of students interested in and learning about social entrepreneurship. There are now social entrepreneurship modules in Trinity College Dublin, the Michael Smurfit Graduate School of Business and Dublin City University. Social entrepreneurship is typically finding its way into business schools, but should be part of curricula across all social sciences and the arts as well. While studying the theory is valuable, experiential learning is critical and social business competitions across every third level campus are one example of a way to multiply the number of social innovators.

Entrepreneurs are widely considered the innovators of society, but fostering intrapreneurial talent within organisations is also critical. Government and public servants are in a powerful position to bring about transformative change across all social sectors, but the innovative capacity of public servants remains largely untapped. They are dogged by bureaucracy and a culture that punishes mistakes and avoids risk. The media and opposition parties carefully pore over how taxpayers money is spent. Any wastage makes the newspaper headlines. This accountability is critical, but we must also recognise the need to allow public servants and politicians to make mistakes. We have created a culture that stifles creativity, innovation and risk taking within the public service, ensuring business as usual from one government to the next. Who wants to work in this culture? How frustrating this must be for the many public servants with a true commitment to serve. The challenges we face demand innovation in all sectors of society, not business as usual. We must allow everyone to make mistakes if we are to foster an innovation culture in the public service. This is good use of taxpayer's money.

'Nearly every problem has been solved by someone, somewhere. [...] The challenge of the 21st century is to find out what works and scale it up' (Bill Clinton). Many of the solutions to Ireland's social and environmental problems exist across the world but many don't find their way here – this is true for any country in the world. Each new innovation consumes entrepreneurial and leadership capacity, as well as time and financial resources. At the same time, relevant innovations that have proven their effectiveness elsewhere in the world are too often untapped. Importing proven innovations leverages knowledge and technologies developed elsewhere, enabling us to achieve goals with less leadership resources, at higher speed, a lower cost and a higher probability of success. To solve social problems in a timely and cost effective manner, Ireland should systematically seek out and import the most innovative ideas and institutions from around the world, just as we have done so successfully in business. Systematically importing social innovations is an area where Ireland can lead the world. *Roots of Empathy* represent just one example – a Canadian innovation we will import to Ireland to assist with several social challenges.

Demand for the talent and ideas of the world's leading social innovators remains low, because the opportunity has not yet been recognised. Countries who execute first and best will have access to the world's leading social innovators and their ideas. There is no shortage of innovative ideas but the incentives and supports offered to social entrepreneurs to scale beyond regional or national boundaries are non-existent by comparison to the corporate sector. Think of the incentives and supports Ireland provided through the IDA to a Google or Intel in expanding to Ireland. The supports/incentives required for social entrepreneurs to scale their ideas and organisations to Ireland and elsewhere include finance and access to local networks – an innovation brokerage. With the biggest social innovation pool in the world, Ashoka – the world's largest association of social entrepreneurs, is well placed to demonstrate to government and civil society how to import social innovation. We are piloting in Ireland a programme called *The Localizer* that is attracting a selection of the world's leading social entrepreneurs to Ireland, importing innovative solutions that will tackle some of Ireland's entrenched social challenges.

Social entrepreneurship was an unknown term in Ireland five years ago. While awareness of social entrepreneurship and social innovation has grown broadly, understanding of the value, impact and potential is low and the task of educating people remains. This communication responsibility falls to several organisations and the media. We need to continue to celebrate role models, not just social entrepreneurs, but also leading intrapreneurs who are leading change within the public service, business and citizen sector organisations. The recent 'Ideas Campaign' and 'Your Country, Your Call' competitions have highlighted a little of the untapped problem solving creativity in Ireland. There is value in asking people for their ideas, but why not their changemaking talents as well? What we need are more people executing innovative solutions. The next evolution of these competitions should be a challenge to change your country – a national call for all changemaking talent to step forward and execute new innovations on the ground, in practice.

Government and the public service have not yet embraced the potential in Ireland. Social entrepreneurs are a resource that should make them one of the public sectors' main sparring partners in the coming years. The public services desperately need innovators and entrepreneurs, inside and outside, who can deliver breakthrough innovation: new ways to meet social needs, and new non-governmental resources. More social value at lower cost is one of the primary value propositions. Government's role should be to provide the infrastructure for social entrepreneurship to flourish. Many of Ireland's leading business entrepreneurs, including Dermot Desmond and Denis O'Brien and companies such as NTR and Guinness, have already recognized the potential and are investing finance and expertise. Several European countries, with Britain in the lead, have for more than ten years been working on national strategies for social entrepreneurship. Within the EU context, the European Commission President Jose Manuel Barroso has put social innovation on the agenda for tomorrow's Europe. Speaking to the Bureau of European Policy Advisers in January 2009, the European Commission President said: 'The financial and economic crisis makes creativity and innovation in general and social innovation in particular, even more important to foster sustainable growth, secure jobs and boost competitiveness.' Later that same year, in a consultation paper for EU 2020, he added, 'Growth, sustainable public finances, tackling climate change, social inclusion, a strengthened industrial base and a vibrant services sector are not alternatives. They reinforce each other. We now need new sources of growth to replace the jobs lost in the crisis.'

Ireland can catch up within three years with a smart strategy based on global best practices coupled with relatively small and focused investments. We should build on the strategy of the innovation taskforce to incorporate social innovation and on the existing infrastructure designed for business, including Enterprise Ireland, the County Enterprise Boards, the IDA and Innovation Centres across the country. Social Innovation should reside within the Department of Enterprise, Trade and Innovation and work in partnership with all key stakeholders.

Financing the transition is obviously critical. Social innovations require finance at all stages of their lifecycle – from research and development through execution, refining and scaling up. The type of finance required ranges from grant, debt to equity finance. There are several organisations providing financial support to social innovators, including social finance institutions such as Clann Credo, social venture funds such as Ashoka and Social Entrepreneurs Ireland, government departments and agencies, foundations including One Foundation, Atlantic Philanthropies and the Iris O'Brien Foundation and corporations such as NTR and Guinness. Despite this, the demand for finance far outstrips supply and most social innovators remain crippled by financial constraints. Several financial holes remain and filling them represents a significant opportunity. Some of the most significant opportunities are outlined below.

The Government has committed significant R&D investments in the Strategy for Science, Technology and Innovation (SSTI). Ireland currently invests 1.6% of GDP in R&D, up from 0.5% ten years ago. The stated target is 3% of GDP. A Social Innovation R&D Fund should be formed as part of new iterations of SSTI, focused on research and development of new innovations across education, health, economic development, civic participation, human rights and the environment. This could complement or centralise the several agencies already funding research across these fields. These funds would be open to universities, citizen sector organisations, social entrepreneurs, social businesses and intrapreneurial teams within the public services sector.

The US Government recently launched a $50m Social Innovation Fund for grant investments in scaling up the most promising innovations across the citizen sector. The Irish government should create a more ambitious and strategic Social Innovation Fund that provides debt, equity and grant finance to social innovators across all sectors of society and at all stages of development. There is significant opportunity to leverage philanthropic investments, to invest existing resources more strategically and secure additional finance from European Social Innovation Funds.

Philanthropists have played a central role in building the foundations of the innovation society, both in Ireland and internationally. There is considerable opportunity to transition existing and new philanthropic investors to focus on highly leveraged social innovations. Philanthropy Ireland, The Community Foundation for Ireland and private wealth managers among others have a central role to play here.

There are several private social venture funds emerging across Europe that invest debt and equity finance in social innovations using the methodologies from venture capital and private equity though looking for social returns on investment and lower than traditional returns on finance. Many of these funds are looking for investment opportunities internationally and there is scope to attract these funds to invest in Ireland. These funds are being created by professional investors from the venture capital and private equity industries and also by private banks such as Deutsche Bank. As well as attracting international investors, there is considerable potential to create private social venture funds in Ireland, offering several different products and services to social innovators.

As the social innovation field develops in size and sophistication there will be scope to develop a social stock exchange in Ireland which is currently being tested and refined by several organisations around the world – most notably in Brazil where there are over fifty social businesses listed on an exchange. Nobel laureate Muhamad Yunus, one of the world's leading social innovators, pioneer of the micro finance movement and founder of Grameen Bank, is advocating for the creation of a Social Stock Exchange for non loss, non dividend social businesses, starting with listings on existing exchanges and subsequently creating an entirely new framework for a Social Stock Exchange. The two first and critical steps will be the creation of new legal frameworks for social businesses in Ireland and the development of useful measurement tools for social innovation and social return on investment, based on international research and experience.

A valuable next step in building an innovation society will be the creation of a National Taskforce on Social Innovation to include all of the key stakeholders and build and execute a collective vision, plan and policy framework for Social Innovation in Ireland. In multiplying the number of empathetic, creative and resourceful innovators across Ireland, we can create a society that is capable of solving social and environmental challenges whenever and wherever they might arise.

CHAPTER NINE

Justice
The Future of Penal Policy in Ireland

Liam Herrick

Crime and how it is punished is undoubtedly a political and social issue of considerable controversy and public interest. However, it is fair to say that the area has been characterised by traditional neglect by policy-makers and academia. One simple historical reason for this is the low level of recorded crime experienced in the State for the first 40 years after independence. In fact, despite periods of political instability, the level of crime consistently dropped after 1922 leading to a reduction in Garda numbers and a record low prison population of 373 in 1956. During this period strikingly little political or media attention was devoted to the prison system or criminal justice policy more generally. A significant caveat to this penal moderation was the extremely high use of other closed institutions such as mental hospitals, industrial schools and Magdalene laundries. Ireland chose not to imprison, but that certainly did not mean that we did not detain.

Significant social changes in the 1960s and 1970s saw major increases in many categories of crime and unprecedented levels of public concern about the issue. However, the main thrust of policy in relation to punishment at that time, and since then, has centred on consistently expanding the prison system. Scientific input into policy-making has been conspicuous by its absence, with criminology acutely underdeveloped as an academic discipline in Ireland until very recently. The Department of Justice and Law Reform has traditionally had a very limited research capacity and while a National Crime Council was established in 1999, it was abolished again as part of wider spending cuts in 2008. From time to time, government-led reviews of the penal system were carried out, among them the Whitaker Report on Reform of the Prison System (1985); the Department of Justice's

strategy document 'Management of Offenders' (1994); the report of the National Crime Forum (1998); and the NESF Report
on the Reintegration of Prisoners (2002). These initiatives made
many positive recommendations for legislative and policy
change, but few have been implemented.

In response to public concern around drug crime and organised crime, a large volume of new legislation has been introduced
since the early 1990s. This has been largely reactive in nature
and often enacted without proper consideration by the Oireachtas
through use of the parliamentary 'guillotine'. Much of this legislative and policy response has mimicked the approaches taken
in the United Kingdom and the United States, albeit usually
after some delay and on a smaller scale. A steady increase in
Ireland's prison population since the 1960s has accelerated during this period with our prison population increasing from 2,400
in 1997 to over 4,300 today, with projections of this figure reaching 5,000 by end 2010. The reasons behind this increase have not
been properly analysed; it is not evident that crime is rising, but
there is clear evidence that more people are being brought before the courts and longer sentences are being provided for in
law and being handed down by the judiciary.

At the same time, the public are rightly concerned about the
failure of our crime policies. State responses to a number of specific types of crime seem inadequate. Reoffending rates are high
among our released prisoners and there are clear problems with
recidivist offenders in certain categories of relatively minor
crime. A tendency to legislate rather than address practical issues of crime detection and prevention has undermined public
confidence. Promises to 're-balance' the criminal justice system
from the suspect to the victim of crime have proved empty and
misguided, with recent responses focusing on sentencing and
the fair trial rights of suspects, when all evidence points to crime
prevention and detection as being the most important areas to
address.

There is an urgent need for the development of a new and
more coherent policy for the punishment of crime in Ireland,
one based on clear principles and informed by solid evidence of
what works in reducing crime and creating a safer society. In the
past there has been a temptation to mimic failed crime policies

from the United Kingdom or the United States. Now that both of those systems are undergoing crises and fundamental restructuring of their penal system, an opportunity is emerging to develop a uniquely Irish penal policy before rather than after our prison system expands beyond manageable levels, as has happened in both of those jurisdictions. There is great potential for a smaller, more efficient and more effective penal system. The first step in developing such a policy is to set out clear goals and principles.

Firstly, there is no integrated crime policy which sets out how the various elements and agencies of the criminal justice system should relate to one another and there is very little clarity as to how crime policy is linked to wider social policy objectives. Rising prisoner numbers are placing an increasing financial burden on the State at a time of great need in other areas of social spending. As David Cameron has stated in a British context, governments now have no choice but to advance a reform agenda, as the cost of high levels of incarceration are politically unjustifiable. Whereas the dramatic increases in imprisonment in Britain under Thatcher, Major and especially Blair can be tracked to an ideological attachment to punishment and 'being tough on crime', it might be suggested that Ireland has instead almost sleepwalked into our own particular prison crisis due to official neglect and a lack of deliberate action. During the years of economic boom, the primary response of successive Irish governments to concerns around crime was to build more prisons and recruit more Gardaí. This can be seen as using resources as a substitute for policy, rather than representing any thought-out response to a social problem. Since the mid-90s building more prison spaces, rather than lowering crime, has been presented as a political achievement in itself.

There is a growing body of evidence which indicates that the redistribution of resources towards prevention and early intervention strategies can have long-term economic benefits by reducing future crime and offending behaviour in a cheaper and more effective manner. In particular, investing resources in a scientific manner on proven initiatives with groups at high risk of being drawn into crime has been demonstrated in the United States to produce significant economic dividends. The resulting benefits to society include a reduction in the need for imprisonment. In this regard, the failures of Irish government policy and the lack of investment in services around drug misuse, mental health and childcare can be seen to have contributed to our growing crime problems. As these issues explain important aspects of crime, it is also in these areas that solutions to patterns of crime can be found, rather than from within the criminal justice system.

Secondly, we are committed to the principle of imprisonment as a last resort. IPRT believes that the harm caused by imprisonment should be ameliorated by minimising its use to cases where public safety or the requirements of justice dictate that no other sanctions would be appropriate. Ireland's historic approach to punishing crime is based on the centrality of the prison in our justice system. There is sometimes a need to use detention to protect society and to punish the most serious offenders, but prison is a wasteful and unnecessary option in many cases and it should not be the default sanction in our justice system. With a small number of exceptions, the response of the Irish criminal justice system to the most serious crime and to those who default on fines or commit road traffic offences is the same: detention in medium security prisons. There is growing international acceptance that the effective resourcing of community sanctions offers a cheaper and more effective way of punishing and preventing many categories of crime.

The single biggest factor determining prison population size is sentencing law and practice. IPRT believes that greater transparency and consistency of sentencing can be achieved while retaining the proper independence of the judiciary. Presumptive and mandatory sentencing regimes have a corrosive effect on the criminal justice system, increasing the numbers of people incarcerated, removing necessary judicial discretion and frustrating proportionate sentencing. The most important recent development in this regard is section 15A of the Misuse of Drugs Act (through an amendment introduced in 2006), which provides for ten years as the minimum standard sentence for being in possession of illegal drugs with a value of €13,000 or more for sale or supply. This presumptive sentencing regime is having a significant effect on the size of the prison population, although it is less clear what impact it is having on the scale of the trade in illegal drugs or on senior figures in that trade. A long overdue cost-benefit analysis of this provision and its effects might be very illuminating.

We have identified a number of categories of prisoners that could be completely or largely diverted from the prison system immediately and we have also identified changes to sentencing law and practice that will have a long-term effect in this regard, the prevalence of very short sentences being imposed at the District Court level being a particularly problematic aspect of our penal system. There is much international and domestic evidence that such sentences are counter-productive and present significant administrative difficulties for the prison system. The commitment in the revised Programme for Government to 'ensure that prison is the option of last resort for non-serious crime' in general, and specifically the measures proposed in the Fines Bill 2009 and recent initiatives to end the use of imprisonment for civil debt, are most welcome. In this regard, the operation of the Fines Act 2010 must be monitored to ensure that it succeeds in reducing the practice of imprisonment for non-payment of fines.

The introduction of a statutory provision which would oblige judges to exhaust all alternatives before imprisoning someone in the District Court, as is provided for young offenders under section 96 of the Children Act 2001, is a key element. This should be accompanied by an obligation on sentencing judges at the District Court level to provide written explanations of all custodial sentences. We do not believe that there is a need to create new or more complicated community sanctions options at the point of sentence. However, making diversion a reality requires resources to be invested in the Probation Service to administer schemes such as the Community Service Order Scheme. Legislation and resources may not be enough to change judicial practice, so dialogue with the judiciary and collation of sentencing practice across the country will provide the necessary evidence base to allow more informed sentencing.

A critical area of application in this regard is the area of youth justice, not only because of the devastating effect of crime and detention on young people, but also because of the wider significance of youth justice policy for the adult criminal justice system. On the positive side, the Children Act 2001 and the National Youth Justice Strategy provide a solid framework for the progressive reform of youth justice policy and practice. The issue here is one of implementation – if the existing strategy is supported it will provide the basis for the continuing decline in the need to detain children. The role of the Garda as the first contact that young people have with the justice system is crucial in forming attitudes to crime and justice among young people. The continuing growth of the Garda Diversion Programme is a major success story in preventing young people getting drawn into the criminal justice system. This programme must continue to receive appropriate support and resources.

There is potential for even greater levels of diversion away from detention in cases where young people are before the courts. Delays in prosecution may sometimes be inevitable; however, in some instances delays can mean that opportunities are missed to respond to offending behaviour before it becomes more serious. Delays and the need for detention on remand can both be reduced by practical measures such as the case management system being implemented by the Gardaí in Dublin at present. Unfortunately, we still have a high rate of detention of children on remand and long delays in bringing young people before the court. The continuing use of St Patrick's Institution for the imprisonment of children is deeply disturbing and constitutes a clear violation of Ireland's human rights obligations. It should cease immediately. This has been promised for many years, but each year a new generation of young boys are committed to a damaging and dangerous environment.

Finally, our penal system must fully respect standards of human rights in line with Ireland's obligations under international law and the Constitution. Respect for human rights standards is not some abstract or idealistic aspiration. At one level, Ireland has voluntarily and democratically, through the Oireachtas, undertaken solemn obligations to the international community to respect certain rights such as the prohibition on inhuman and degrading treatment. At a more profound level, our Constitution sets out a social contract in which everyone in the State is guaranteed certain fundamental and basic rights including rights to dignity and to bodily integrity. Persistent and clear violations of human rights go to the core of our democracy and our prisons are the site of some of the most pressing human rights issues in the State.

Notwithstanding the resources available over the past decade, the emphasis has been on expansion rather than modernisation, which has left us facing a shortage of resources with a system that is desperately antiquated in many places and chronically overcrowded throughout. The physical conditions in our older prisons are completely unacceptable and have been the subject of consistent criticism from international bodies. Overcrowding, rising violence and demeaning physical conditions in our prisons have contributed to institutions which are likely to exacerbate rather than address criminality. In short, our older prisons are an international disgrace, with the Council of Europe Committee for the Prevention of Torture describing them as 'unsafe' for staff or prisoners, and the Inspector of Prisons directing that Mountjoy should not be operating at its current levels of overcrowding 'because of [his] serious concerns for safety or life'.

Indeed, the Inspector of Prisons and international human rights bodies have categorically stated that overcrowding is the most important risk factor in relation to prisoner violence and self-harm, not only exacerbating problems such as violence and drug use in prisons but also undermining attempts at rehabilitation of offenders. The Inspector has already recommended safe custody limits for certain prisons and there are a number of practical measures that can be taken to reduce overcrowding in the short term. The continuing absence of an independent complaints mechanism, such as a Prisoner Ombudsman, within the prison system is a major weakness of the system, as is the absence of an effective system for the investigation of deaths in custody.

While the current outlook for a prison system that is increasing at 14% a year is bleak, with political leadership and vision the serious problems facing the Irish prison system can be addressed separately from the issue of prison expansion. Ireland's recent prison-building programmes were initiated in a situation when little data on prison populations was publicly available, and certainly not published. In other jurisdictions, complex models for projecting prison population trends are employed and are made accessible to members of the public. The replacement or refurbishment of old prison stock can be pursued without the huge costs that would be involved in the proposed scale of prison expansion that would be incurred if the Thornton Hall and Kilworth projects go ahead as planned.

The proper design and planning of institutions should be based on detailed data on demographic trends, including age and gender, in the prisons and in the general population. The key policy question to be addressed here is whether to continue moving towards a smaller number of larger institutions. The concentration of most of our prisons in the Dublin region presents a further difficulty, particularly for families visiting loved ones. A geographical breakdown of offenders and prisoners should be used to identify the areas of the country where prisons might most usefully be located, incorporating the principle of 'localism' which would recommend more small prisons rather than larger institutions which are more expensive and more difficult to manage. A detailed picture of the current prison population – types of offenders, length of sentences being served – should also inform the general security classification needs of our prisons addressing issues such as the need for an open prison for women and the need for a specialised prison for young adult offenders.

Ultimately, the size of the prison population in a given society is determined by a complex series of factors, but is predicated in the first instance on a political choice. The long-term direction of prison policy must be informed by a decision about the number of prisoners Ireland wants to have. We believe that the guiding principle in making this choice should be that imprisonment should be used sparingly and should be focused on the detention of those who commit serious crime or pose a real threat to public safety. If diversion in youth justice policy continues to be supported, if changes are introduced in sentencing law to divert offenders, and if community sanctions are properly resourced, then IPRT believes that prison expansion will no longer be necessary and our current prison population can be reduced.

CHAPTER TEN

Sport and Fitness
The Case for Child Friendly Fitness Testing and Monitoring

Eamonn Henry/James Nolan

Introduction

In this chapter we set out medium to long term policy measures that would support improved physical fitness of children through their primary and post primary years. Changes in our education system will be essential for the realisation of this objective. Complementary measures across a number of government departments to support a national prioritisation of physical fitness among children will also be necessary, as will a national cultural shift in relation to its importance.

More specifically, we make the case for the annual mass testing of children across Ireland to establish the nation's 'fitness age' and to monitor, over a fifteen to twenty year period, trends to the established time bound baseline. To demonstrate the value of such an approach the story of the FAST Kids pilot project in Co Offaly is told and one possible model for testing is outlined.

Societal challenges

Preventing obesity and its resultant consequences is one of the major health challenges facing Ireland. Childhood obesity in Ireland has reached epidemic levels with a third of girls and a fifth of boys overweight.[1] The Report of the National Task Force on Obesity in 2005 estimated that over 300,000 children in Ireland are currently overweight or obese and this is projected to increase by 10,000 annually. The report also states that 18% of adults are obese and 39% are overweight. It estimates that the obesity epidemic is responsible for approximately 2,000 premature deaths in Ireland per annum and contributes to hypertension, Type 2 diabetes, cardiovascular disease, osteoarthritis, some types of cancer and many other disorders. The implications

1. Regan (2008)

of these statistics on the overall well being of our population and the increasing strain that rising obesity levels will put on our health services must not be underestimated.

While a range of interventions are necessary to combat the existing problem among all affected groups, preventative measures need to be in place at an early age and continued throughout the life cycle in order to build a sustained culture of healthy living. Left unchecked, young children will imitate the behaviour and habits of an adult population which has moved in a very unhealthy direction. The first intervention proposed here, and outlined in greater detail further on, is the establishment of a concept called the national 'fitness age' as a time bound measure of children's fitness. Once established, striving for improvements to the national 'fitness age' will be essential.

One of the major anomalies concerning sport and physical activity as a public policy strategy to prevent childhood obesity is that research data from the Irish Sports Council and the ESRI suggests that children are actually playing more sport than previous generations and that the relationship between weight and the playing of sport is weak.[2] However, other Sports Council and ESRI research[3] concerning adult participation states that 'eliminating physical inactivity would result in 15-39% less coronary heart disease, 33% less stroke, 12% less hypertension, 12-15% less diabetes, 22-23% less colon cancer, 5-12% less breast cancer and 18% less osteoporotic fractures' – all conditions that present a risk to an overweight and obese population. For this reason we contend that public policy in relation to children's well being must firstly be focused on their fitness levels and taking them to the start of adulthood in the best possible physical condition attainable.

We believe there are increased opportunities for children to play competitive sport from as young as five and six years. However, while some children are being recruited into mainstream sport at this age, inadequate attention is being given to the development of core fundamental movement skills, a point that was highlighted to us by local research in 2008. Moreover,

2. Fahey et al (2005)
3. Fahey et al (2004)

some competitive sports structures can be inappropriate for young children, resulting in early drop out. The continual focus on winning in some quarters (even if it is only for the county under-8 championship) often results in the segregation of children at training, quite often unintentional on the part of coaches and leaders. 'Put the big lad in the goals so he doesn't have to run about too much' is not an uncommon approach. Research can capture that the 'big lad' was involved in sport and participated in PE at school – it might not capture that he got little or no physical benefit from his experience.

Even with 'regular size' children involved in mainstream sport, there can also be a lack of adequate physical activity on two counts. Firstly, those that play sport today are normally dropped to and picked up from training venues by car. Thus the physical activity they receive is confined to the actual training session for the sport. Previous generations usually walked, ran or cycled to and from training sessions.[4] Secondly, in much of Ireland, opportunities for children to participate in sport are largely confined to the spring and summer months. Therefore physical activity and fitness is not sustained throughout the year.

The gendered nature of participation is a further area for concern. The socialisation and expectations of girls and boys are different in relation to sport. The opportunities created for both sexes are unequal and first call on sports facilities is ordinarily afforded to mens' and boys' teams. This results in fewer girls taking up sport in the first instance and drop out occurring for girls at a younger age.

Research by the Irish Sports Council and the ESRI[5] further suggests that income status and advancement through the education system are additional factors that will determine the likelihood of individuals remaining involved in sport and physical activity in their adult lives.

The present structure of the education system and curriculum

---

4. In the case of the authors of this paper, both lived over 2 miles from their local training venues. Eamonn contends that James' hardest training as a child was running to and from the club sessions and this is what gave him the endurance capacity to win so many underage national titles.
5. Lunn (2007)

also creates significant barriers to participation. While very high expectations are placed on schools and teachers, these are not backed up with adequate resourcing or time allocations. The commitment and experience of teachers varies from school to school within the primary system as does the allocation of concessionary time to physical education and the involvement of schools in extra curricular sport (for boys and girls). A number of post-primary schools do not engage PE teachers and there is a conflict for children participating in sport in the run up to state examinations.

A shift in policy
In our view, policy discussions need to centre around the following issues:
- Core changes, primarily facilitated by the education system, needed to create the cultural shift necessary to develop a young fit population.
- Supportive measures that can be facilitated by inter-departmental prioritisation of physical fitness.

Core changes needed to support the development of a young fit population
There is a need to position education, in conjunction with the Irish Sports Council, to measure, monitor and inform society of the fitness levels of our children. This could include the following:
- Establishing the 'fitness age' of the country through mass testing and fitness monitoring of children within the primary school system, complemented by inclusive mass participation programmes to improve fitness.
- Expanding the testing and monitoring of children into the post-primary system.
- Introducing PE as a state examination at Junior and Leaving Certificate level in the medium term with a high proportion of marks available being based on the attained fitness and sports specific skills of the students.
- Introducing changes to college/career entry for specific study programmes and jobs[6] to give recognition of attainment in PE examinations.

6. e.g. sport, health based studies, teaching, defence and security.

Establishing and Monitoring the Nation's 'Fitness Age'

Educators have the ability to test the functional literacy and numerical abilities of children and determine their performance relative to age. Health professionals know the appropriate weights, heights, heart rates, hearing and vision for babies, toddlers and young children at various stages in their development. However, we do not currently use any universal measures to determine the capacity of children to perform a range of physical exertions relative to their age in order to determine if intervention is necessary. This chapter advocates the establishment of such a universal measure and a public policy for its adaptation within all primary schools (i.e. schools being required to conduct annual fitness tests of pupils, with results being notified to a central body – most likely the Irish Sports Council).

In the absence of a public policy that supports the monitoring *en masse* of children's fitness levels, it is still possible for individual schools, clubs and bodies with a larger catchment (e.g. Local Sports Partnerships, county and regional structures of governing bodies of sport) to test children aged from 7 to 12 years in a fun-filled environment against data which has been collected in the UK. Using a system called the *Sportshall Decathlon*,[7] developed by George Bunner,[8] children undertake ten consecutive tests where each performance is converted to a points score and added to all other nine test scores. The child's score is then plotted on a fitness monitoring chart against his/her age and sex. It can be immediately shown whether the child's score is:

- In the top 5% of all children
- In the top 15% but not in the top 5%
- Above average but not in the top 15%
- Below average but not in the lowest 25%
- In the lowest 25% but not in the lowest 5%
- In the lowest 5% of all children

7. For further information on the *Sportshall Decathlon* and the Fitness Monitoring Chart see *Sportshall Athletics*, (3rd edition, 2007), by George Bunner MBE, edited by Ivan Bunner and published by Eveque. All *Sportshall* programmes referred to in this chapter were developed by Mr Bunner with the copyright being held by Eveque.

8. Mr Bunner began *Sportshall Athletics* in 1976 and has been continually developing and improving innovative programmes for children ever since. In 2002 he received his MBE for over 25 years of service to athletics.

The advantages of this test[9] are:

- A universal system of activities can be used for the mass monitoring of fitness.
- It does not require professional medical administration.
- It focuses on the attainment of a fitness outcome rather than a 'body size' outcome.
- It is concerned with the individual child where s/he is at (i.e. it gives each child its own starting point on which to improve and incorporates a series of targets that the child can strive to achieve).
- It is fun and inclusive for children thereby offering the potential for mass participation.
- It is easy for teachers, volunteers and sports leaders to administer.
- It can identify individuals, geographic locations and pockets of concern in need of intervention.

It should be noted that the test is best approached as a 'challenge' and provides a fun yet competitive programme for children to gauge their own improvement. Annual award schemes for improvements in fitness and agility should be incorporated into a testing programme and the test results should be centrally administered. In an Irish context serious consideration will need to be given to interventions for individuals and locations where mass testing highlights children falling well below expected norms.

Testing and Monitoring of Fitness Norms for Secondary School Children
Once established at primary school level, a similar system should be developed within the post-primary system in order that children learn to continue the culture of self challenge through the education system. Within the post-primary system, the PE curriculum should accommodate the annual testing. Provision will have to be made for a test which reflects the physiological development of post-primary children, provides for windows of opportunity for development of strength and is

---

9. A further advantage of the tests is that they can be used to identify emerging talent. This is not the primary function of the tests and they should not be used for this. However, the tests can be used as a mechanism to encourage talented children to stay with sport.

gender specific. We anticipate that the establishment of a fitness baseline for post-primary children in Ireland will show a widening of test scores between boys and girls.

PE as an exam subject
When annual testing and fitness monitoring have become the norm for children within education, and adequate data is available to plot the 'fitness age' of the nation, consideration has to be given to making PE a state exam subject. As an exam subject 50%-70% of available marks should be given for a mandatory physical fitness test and the execution of a choice of sports specific skills. The theory aspect of the curriculum should provide students with a level of awareness and understanding that will inform life choices in relation to sport and physical activity.

The physical tests would need to be both age and gender specific and should also accommodate any disability that a student may have. These tests should be time bound, based on the baseline of fitness determined for secondary schools referred to above. In this way the objective of continuing to improve fitness throughout second level becomes attainable for the vast majority of the population.

It is recommended that this would be compulsory up to Junior Certificate level and optional for the Leaving Certificate. However, Leaving Certificate students should continue to be allocated PE time during each school week. Likewise there should be an incentive (as outlined below) to continue with PE as an exam subject up to the Leaving Certificate.

PE as a study and career pathway
To help realise the culture of activity throughout one's time in school, and beyond, there should be incentives to perform above average in physical activity tests and examinations. Across government departments, consideration should be given to incentives for those taking and performing above average in Physical Education. Incentivised entry to specific college courses and careers in the following sectors should also be considered:

- Sports programmes
- The health sector

- Education and teaching
- State defence and security

Supportive Measures of Other Government Departments
With a national prioritisation of children's fitness, there are a range of complementary measures that could be put in place by other government departments and statutory bodies to support the attainment of this goal. For example:

- A national programme to complement the work of schools would need to be developed by the Irish Sports Council and delivered locally through the network of Local Sports Partnerships.
- The Irish Sports Council should use its influence with governing bodies of sport to implement a similar approach within their training programmes.
- The Health Promotion Section of the HSE should ensure that targeted measures are in place at post-primary level to support teenagers in attaining the recommended levels of physical activity outlined in the National Guidelines.[10]
- The Department of Education and Skills, in conjunction with the Department of Tourism, Culture and Sport, must establish a mechanism to ensure that school halls and sports facilities are available during out of school hours and at weekends for children's sport and fitness programmes.
- The Department of Community, Equality and Gaeltacht Affairs, through its support of Local Development Companies, CDPs and Family Resource Centres, should prioritise a number of localised training options in every county in Ireland to ensure that a local pool of volunteers are in place to support delivery of inclusive participation programmes for children. Likewise bodies that manage labour market initiatives[11] should prioritise a number of places on each of their schemes specifically for trained personnel to assist in the delivery of children's programmes.

---

10. Get Ireland Active: National Guidelines on Physical Activity for Ireland (2009)
11. e.g. Community Employment Scheme managed by FÁS and the Rural Social Scheme managed by Local Development Companies for the Department of Social Protection.

The FAST Kids story

The underlying belief in the value of interventions to tackle children's core fundamental fitness and the importance of testing to confirm success is based on our experience in establishing and delivering the FAST Kids project (i.e. children having Fun, while improving Agility, Speed and Technical proficiency) in Co Offaly.

The story of the FAST Kids project in Co Offaly can be traced back to 2007. Pamela Kelleghan, a graduate of the Business and Sports Management programme at the Athlone Institute of Technology was on placement with the Offaly Sports Partnership. In the course of her work, Ms Kelleghan observed that a large number of children had very poor co-ordination, with some having an irrational fear of attempting simple balance exercises (e.g. balancing on one foot on a balance beam 3 inches off the ground).

To establish if there was a need for concern the Partnership organised for children in the county to be tested in 2008 using the *Sportshall Pentathlon*. In this challenge, which is similar to the *Sportshall Decathlon*, children could achieve one of seven possible colour awards based on cumulative scores achieved across the five activities tested (with gold, silver and bronze being the highest, blue and green the mid level award and yellow and orange the lowest). Tests were carried out by Emma Bunworth, a fourth year student of Sport and Leisure at the Tralee Institute of Technology. A total of 727 children from across 18 schools in the county were tested (representing over 15% of school going children from the age cohort).

Of the children tested, none achieved the gold or silver awards, 3 (0.4%) achieved the bronze, while over 80% were ranked in the two lowest categories. The research concluded that, as a matter of priority, Offaly Sports Partnership needed to develop and implement programmes that would improve children's basic agility.

On receipt of Ms Bunworth's study findings, the Partnership established contact with the programme developers in the UK who proved very supportive in providing advice and analysis. A line of communication also opened up between the authors of this chapter, Offaly Sports Partnership co-ordinator Eamonn

Henry and James Nolan who, at that time, was based in South Africa. As an established elite international athlete, James had travelled extensively and had witnessed a number of programmes in various countries being used to introduce children to sport. The common threads running through the most successful ones, as James had observed, were enjoyment, variety, and the teaching of movement in a playful way. James developed a strong desire to introduce similar approaches in Ireland when he would eventually retire from international athletics.

The Partnership piloted an indoor winter programme of *Sportshall Athletics* in the county, culminating in an inter-school event for 6 schools and approximately 300 children. This programme was positively received and the Partnership committed to keeping it alive and trying to expand it despite limited resources.

Fate intervened in a somewhat cruel manner to ensure that the programme was delivered in 2009. A recurring injury forced James to retire from international athletics and to return home from South Africa. His retirement coincided with a call from Social Entrepreneurs Ireland for applications to its annual round of awards. An application was submitted and James was awarded a small 'Level 1' award to establish FAST Kids and to show that international fitness programmes for children were transferable to Ireland.

In the autumn/winter of 2009 the FAST Kids programme was introduced to 20 schools in Offaly with over 1,600 children participating. Over 1,100 children participated in inter-schools fun competitions based on the universal rules for *Sportshall Athletics*. James delivered a ten week intervention into one of the 20 participating schools (Daingean National School) and had the 83 children from 4th to 6th class tested using the *Sportshall Pentathlon* test. The results from this showed substantial improvement when compared with the 2008 baseline. 25% of pupils obtained the upper level awards, 66% the mid way awards and 9% ranked in the lowest categories (no pupil placed in the very lowest category).

These results confirm that international children's programmes of good practice are transferable to Ireland. They also demonstrate how the agility and fitness of large numbers of children (girls and boys) can be enhanced with the correct interventions.

Conclusion

The use of fitness testing and monitoring has been critical to the success of our work to date and provides us with the belief and conviction that this approach needs to be expanded to a wider audience of children.

Improving and sustaining to adulthood, the fitness levels of current and future generations of Irish children (girls and boys) has to be a public policy priority. Poor physical fitness needs to be tackled with the same seriousness that we hope society would tackle illiteracy among children or falling standards in mathematics. A national policy on children's fitness will be necessary to achieve maximum impact and as a society we need to recognise that having a functionally fit population of children is as important to our future as having a functionally literate one.

References:

Fahey, T., Delaney, L. and Gannon, B. (2005), *School Children and Sport in Ireland*, Dublin: Economic and Social Research Institute.

Fahey, T., Layte, R. and Gannon, B. (2004), *Sports Participation and Health Among Adults in Ireland*, Dublin: Economic and Social Research Institute.

Department of Health and Children (2009), *Get Ireland Active: National Guidelines on Physical Activity for Ireland*, Department of Health and Children, Health Service Executive.

Lunn, P. (2007), Fair Play? *Sport and Social Disadvantage in Ireland*, Dublin: Economic and Social Research Institute.

Regan, M. (2008), *Child obesity crisis hits epidemic levels*, Irish Examiner, 1 April.

CHAPTER ELEVEN

Spirituality and Religion
When Faith Grows Up!

Diarmuid Ó Murchú

According to the 2006 Census in Ireland, a mere 4.4% ticked the 'no religion' box. At the height of the cult of the Celtic Tiger, most Irish people still retained a degree of religious sentiment. Although money and wealth had become the foundational values in many people's lives, a sense of spiritual attachment prevailed. Only a few thousand people had opted out of religion completely, and I suspect some would still wish to be identified as spiritual, although they consciously reject religion.

There is another face to the religious face of Ireland captivated in Malachi O'Doherty's *Empty Pulpits*. It is the nostalgia for a mythic past, rapidly fading into the recesses of history. Yet, it is strangely alive, thanks to the furore about clerical abuse, and the strange dynamics whereby Irish people want to keep the priest as a central focus of their faith and religion. There may be empty churches (although amazingly some are still quite full), but there certainly are not empty pulpits, despite the haemorrhaging of vocations in recent decades.

On 19 August 2006, Archbishop Diarmuid Martin addressed the General Humbert Summer School in Killala and alluded to the fact that some schools in Dublin city now have a cultural mix of up to 100 nationalities. He complemented the educational system, specifically the teachers, for the richness and vitality of such unity-in-diversity. He suggested that such diversity enhanced rather than undermined the religious inheritance of Ireland while acknowledging the formidable challenges it posed for the cultural and spiritual development of future Ireland.

A Nation in Transition
Up to 1970, Ireland was predominantly an agricultural country,

---

1. O'Doherty (2008)

with agrarian values very much to the fore. When we joined the Common Market in 1973, it was hoped that this would enhance our prospects as a land-based people, but to the contrary, the added incentives from Europe favoured industry and education. Rapidly, we became a highly educated country with significant numbers of young people moving into the burgeoning field of information technology. For much of the 1990s, Ireland was the leading country in pioneering computer software.

Young people did not want to stay on the land; there were too many exciting alternative options. Those who did stay increasingly found it a struggle to survive as the European Union began to multiply bureaucracy that severely restricted the movement of agricultural produce. To survive in farming, one had to be in it on a big scale. In several farming homesteads, people were unable to survive on the income from the land; another job became essential. This move had a significant impact on family life and on local village communities. Traditional faith became associated with Sundays and special occasions; religion did not move in pace with the cultural changes that were happening.

Ireland today is a global cosmopolitan country, and still makes a significant international contribution particularly in Information Technology (IT). In the opening paragraphs above, I highlight the death and possible rebirth of Irish cultural identity. Irish people are still proud of their religious past, although many will not state that explicitly; it is a cultural inheritance that still carries internal weight and meaning. Its significance is likely to recede in the coming years, although I suspect it will morph into other spiritual expressions rather than regress into either atheism or agnosticism.

The Catholic Church will continue to lose impact and influence, felt more intensely while the issue of clerical abuse still lingers. This sensitive and painful issue – for both victims and perpetrators – will persist for quite a few decades. In itself, it is difficult to determine how much it has contributed to the waning of religion in Ireland. As a social scientist, I would attribute the decline to secularisation and the excessive wealth of the 1990s rather than to internal crises of the church. The most severe crisis facing the church within the next decade is how to envisage spiritual and sacramental leadership in the total absence of priests. Ireland is not alone in this predicament – no Catholic country is facing this eventuality with truth and transparency.

The words of Archbishop Diarmuid Martin could be seen as a rally call for the multi-cultural, multi-ethnic, multi-religious Ireland of the future. The diversity is already apparent, and in a natural organic way, an amazing degree of integration has already taken place. Being fundamentally a young population, having been exposed to a range of other places and cultures, foreign settlers have been embraced socially and religiously, even though not always welcome when competing for limited economic and employment resources. On par with every other European country, Ireland will become ever more diverse in its cultural and religious make-up. And in dealing with this relatively new phenomenon, it will be very much a case of learn as we go along.

Despite its strong cultural Catholic image – the one time Island of Saints and Scholars – Ireland has known religious diversity for quite some time. Ever since the 1960s, Irish Sisters, Brothers and Priests have been influenced through international experiences either through missionary-type endeavours, or through renewal programmes in the United States and elsewhere. Beginning in the 1970s, lay people – particularly media-folk and IT workers – also began to travel and interface internationally. This enculturation has impacted on Irish lifestyle and values far more deeply than is generally recognised. Initially, it percolated through to the rank-and-file largely through the influence of television (e.g. the popularity of Gay Byrne's *Late Late Show*) and latterly through computerisation and the transglobal explosion in mass communication.

Nobody in 1970 is likely to have been able to predict the Ireland that exists in 2010. The changes that will happen in the next ten years are likely to be even more momentous. In terms of religion and spirituality, the overt culture still clings onto the naïve notion that the essentials will never change, and that somehow a unifying religious fabric (via the church) will continue to prevail. How we can help each other to transcend that myopia, and how we can educate the nation into more creative alternative thinking – what Edward do Bono one time called, lateral thinking – is probably the single greatest challenge of the next decade. Some of its implications for religion and spirituality I highlight in the remainder of this article.

Ireland's Dark Night

I suggest Ireland is entering a dark night of the soul,[2] a painful paschal journey nobody will wish to undergo, least of all the institutional church itself. I suggest the damning reports on sexual abuse, particularly the Ryan Report of May 2009, mark the beginning of this long journey through the impending desert. The dissolution of the Celtic Tiger is another symptom, already taking a terrible psychological, spiritual – and financial – toll on the people. Mass emigration will probably become the norm once more. And while there will not be a return to the kind of poverty depicted in Frank McCourt's *Angela's Ashes*, survival will be quite a struggle for many folks.

The dark night involves a dying to all we held precious, to that which we deemed to be immortal and impervious to change. In ten years' time it will be abundantly clear that nothing can escape the evolutionary trajectory of birth-death-rebirth. The prospects and hope of a changed, purified and renewed church will be viewed with greater realism, albeit still with shock and disbelief. Clericalised priesthood will be in the throes of death – it probably already is – but nobody wants to acknowledge that fact. Importing foreign clergy is a stop-gap response with no enduring value – a classical example of Elizabeth Kübler-Ross' bargaining, the third stage in the dying process.[3] For the Irish people, that will be the greatest crucifixion of all.

The rebirth into a new sense of faith – and eventually a new way of being church – will also be a slow painful process – largely because the people will not have been prepared for it. Groping our way in the dark, with few useful landmarks, will be our collective desert experience. Confidence in all forms of authority – secular and religious – is likely to reach an all time low. And Kübler-Ross' anger stage may lead to an increase in crime and

2. Moore (2004)
3. Kübler-Ross (1973)

violence. Unfortunately, but predictably, we can expect an increase in addictive behaviour to numb the pain of our collective and personal disenchantment.

By depicting such a gloomy outlook, I run the risk of losing the reader, if I have not already. One of my areas of specialisation is grief therapy, and that is the backdrop to several of my remarks above. Every grief therapist knows how paralysing blocked grief becomes. When an individual, organisation, or nation cannot mourn its losses it is likely to repress its grief, and become numb to the pain and possibility of the dying experience. Even more formidable is the challenge to bury the dead, so that the ghosts don't stay around to haunt us, thus inhibiting our ability to respond creatively to the call of the new.

When managed in a more informed and discerning way, loss, decline and death can be liberating and empowering – but not until we firstly embrace the journey of the dark night. It is not my intention to paint a depressing picture. Rather my hope is to call people to a sense of realism, because that is what generates a true sense of hope. In the words of Vaclav Havel, one time president of the Czech Republic: 'Hope is not the conviction that something will turn out well, but the certainty that something makes sense regardless of how it turns out.' In times of radical change we cannot make sense of our experience without facing honestly that which has to die and fade into history. Not even the Island of Saints and Scholars is impervious to the dark night of the paschal journey!

Cultural Lag
In 1922, an American sociologist, William F. Ogburn, coined the term cultural lag to describe the discrepancies that arise when the monopoly of former beliefs or values is derailed by newly emerging trends and developments. Conventionally, the lag arises due to the tendency of material culture to evolve and change rapidly while non-material culture tends to resist change and remain fixed for a far longer period of time. We see this very clearly in the boom years of the Celtic Tiger. The acquisition of wealth, property and material goods became the new social and spiritual security. Reliance on God, or even reliance on neighbours, faded into the background. Irish contributions to

needy causes around the world still evoked a generous response, but people were contributing out of their excess wealth
rather than from limited resources.

This discrepancy is not unique to Celtic Tiger Ireland. It has
been noted universally: when people's material security is enhanced, religious fervour and practice tends to recede and even
diminish. Conventional religions have evolved mainly from
agrarian cultures, with a strong appeal to the peasantry.
Dependence on God's good favour features strongly, and God is
beseeched at great length in the face of adversity and struggle.
Whether intended or not, the religion becomes a control system,
and people often adopt a passive, dependent role, with unhealthy reliance particularly on authority figures.

Religion fails to keep pace with human growth and development. People learn the teachings of the faith from home and
school, and what they learn as youngsters remains largely un-
changed for the rest of their lives. They are, therefore, ill-pre-
pared to deal with cultural shifts, in which meaning is challenged and understanding of life-issues changes. Initially people may feel guilty about lack of religious fervour, but quite
quickly those feelings abate and the religious values are either
ignored or discarded.

Much more confusing, and psychologically unhealthy, is the
ensuing sense of cultural drift. People may still go to church regularly; echoes of the old allegiance compel them to hold on to
something, even though it may be only twice a year: Christmas
and Easter, and of course, special events such as funerals and
weddings. However, they expect little from church-going, and
even inspiring church services may not strongly impact upon
them. And they certainly will not worry unduly about the
church's moral teachings!

Developmentally, this ambiguous, apathetic space begets its
own unravelling. Young children asking religious questions are
likely to be fobbed off with answers which the parent learned
perhaps 30 years previously. There is little or no recognition that
the child is living in a world of mass information, and deserves a
response congruent with such a world. The parent expects the
school to do the real work on religion and faith, but what can
schooling achieve when the organic foundations of home-life

have been weakened and undermined. Therefore, passing on of the faith veers ever closer to the collapse of meaning. Symbols fail to speak; sacraments begin to feel like archaic rituals. Religion comes to be seen as a Marxist-type opiate of a people who have lost their way.

This is a rather chaotic scenario, a cultural diagnosis, which many Irish people would dispute. More disturbing still, is the perceived irrelevance of religion, in which case people are not even interested in analysing the problem. I offer the above description in the belief that in the years to come, the disillusionment with church and religion will deepen, to a degree that will be difficult to rationalise or deny. Hopefully, then, people might be more transparent and honest in acknowledging the deep malaise that has gripped the country.

Enter Spirituality

All over the world, people tend not to tolerate meaninglessness for too long. As an interim measure they will fall back on a range of compensations, of which drugs, sex, excessive shopping, and various addictions are the contemporary forms. When major religions collapse, the will-to-meaning is likely to explore alternative ways of reclaiming spiritual meaning. Already this development is taking place in Ireland – and some researchers have noted its evolution.[4]

One hears people make statements like: I am spiritual but not religious. Faith in divine guidance is still in place, even for people who are reluctant to use the 'God' word. Those who hunger for spiritual meaning seek out kindred spirits to share experiences, to pray together, and possibly to ritualise significant life-transitions. Initially, this is likely to be quite human-centred, and will evoke strong condemnation from the church as excessively individualistic and lacking in any real sense of community. The communal dimension comes to the fore in social outreach (rather than in communal worship) with, at times, a strong commitment to justice-making on behalf of the marginalised and oppressed, at home and abroad.

The personal and social boundaries are often unclear. A

---

4. e.g., Clarke (2007); Flanagan and Kelly (2004)

'new-age' interest in crystals, tarot cards and Eastern-based religious practices may prevail in some cases, although it certainly is not as widespread as church condemnation often insinuates. Much more to the fore is a new awakening to the sacredness of the land and the God we encounter in nature. Networking around health and well-being (alternative therapies) is another popular expression, with a strong focus on body-mind-spirit integration.

Over the coming years the hunger for a new spirituality is likely to become much more acute in Ireland. The rapidly ageing profile of clergy will leave church practice dilapidated and haphazard; importing priests from other parts of the Christian world is likely to be the disappointing resolution it has proved to be in other parts of the Western world. A growing awareness will arise that the future of faith in Ireland has to become a peoples' prerogative. We can only wait and see if enough brave souls will come forward to catalyse the new movement.

When Faith Grows Up!
It is unlikely that Ireland will sink into becoming an atheistic country. However, church allegiance will continue to wane, and church influence will continue to dwindle. We may still be in the doldrums of that which is fragmenting even ten years hence. There is a slight chance that we will begin to acknowledge what is happening and become proactive in bringing a new spirituality into being. For that to happen, the following three initiatives are likely to prove significant:

1. Adult Faith Development
Catechising the young has been a central feature of evangelisation in Ireland for a long time. We invest heavily in the process, with the naïve expectation that if we get them young enough – and indoctrinate them well – we'll have their faith-allegiance from there on. It is all too obvious that this approach is a disastrous failure. Faith-development belongs primarily to the home; if it is not nurtured well there, all the formal education on earth is not likely to compensate in any significant way.

Over the past few decades we have evidenced several attempts at re-visioning catechetical formation for our youth, and once again the long-term results are not promising. I suggest that the focus for the future needs to be on adults, and not on children or adolescents. All over the Christian world, we need to shift the focus to adult faith development. The organic passing on of a mature and integrated faith can only happen when adults (e.g. parents) have appropriated the faith in a more adult way. Parents will then know – in a more intuitive and informed way – how to pass on the faith to their children – and will not be looking to educational establishments to facilitate the process on their behalf.

I acknowledge that this is a shift of seismic proportion, and I have no idea how it can be activated or implemented in a practical way. But I am in little doubt that it is a major part of a long-term resolution. Genuine mature faith, which is what many people are seeking in the new search for spirituality, is an adult maturing process, requiring adult input, in an adult way, that gets us away from so much of the religious co-dependency we have known for several centuries. The fuller details of this vision are outlined in my book on adult faith.[5]

2. Reclaiming the wisdom of ritual-making
The awakening interest in Celtic Spirituality could well become the focus for a revitalised appreciation and understanding of our faith as a Christian people in Ireland. Even though most of the population now lives in towns and cities, the sacredness and fruitfulness of the land is very much inscribed in our psyches. Several primary schools in Ireland have developed gardens in which young children participate in growing vegetables and fruits. Markets selling home-grown produce have regained popularity in recent years. And there is quite a strong organic gardening movement in Ireland.

One element of Celtic Spirituality that we tend to overlook is the significance of indigenous ritual: the celebrations of the seasons, of the equinoxes, the fertility of the soil, rites of passage to mark various life stages and experiences. Allegations of neopaganism or new-ageism inhibits people from this potentially rich exploration. As a human species we have largely lost our

5. Ó Murchú (2010)

innate capacity for ritual making. We need to reclaim this rich internal capability, particularly as we face a future Ireland of few if any priests. The people themselves will need to re-learn their capacity for ritual making, and sacramental-rituals will need to be reclaimed as people-centred rituals.

An example that springs to mind is that of marriage. According to the official teaching of the Catholic Church, the essence (matter and form) of this sacrament is the consensual contract between both partners made in word and symbol. It is the couple that administers the sacrament for each other. The priest is merely a witness, on behalf of the church. The priest does not marry the couple, they marry one another. The central role which the priest tends to adopt is actually a contradiction of the church's own teaching, denying and subverting a wonderful moment for people's ritual empowerment.

Our Irish ancestors of old enacted several nature-based rituals around the celebration of the seasons and the fertility of nature. This capacity for ritual-making is deep in our national psyche as well as being a wisdom shared by all spiritually endowed peoples. It requires a shift in our awareness along with some bold educational initiatives to reawaken this propensity. Another formidable challenge for the spiritual life of the Irish people that is likely to be much more obvious – and more pressing – in the years ahead.

3. Ethical governance

Responsibility for the moral fibre of the nation, and its people, will need to become a government responsibility of serious weight and professional commitment. At the moment, it is assumed that this is the primary responsibility of the church, but it is an aspect of church life to which many people pay little heed and less attention. This will need to become a government responsibility. And the remit will need to be broader than issues of private personal morality. Ethical standards related to trade and commerce, several aspects of healthcare, care and cultivation of the land in ecologically responsible ways, support structures for family and married life, ethical guidelines for cross-cultural respect (in a growing home-based international community), and some guidelines on religious mutuality in a highly pluralistic society – all will need to be embraced by Irish governments of the future.

The dualistic distinction between the sacred and the secular no longer serves us well. The Ireland of the future will need a more integrated spirituality that can embrace the complex emerging issues of the 21st century. The government of the country will also need to include in its remit responsibility for the spiritual and cultural development of all the people. It will need to encourage, foster and resource a range of experiments for a new sense of spiritual empowerment, and it will need to set in place structures to adjudicate what is truly life-giving over and above what may be ideologically-motivated.

These three suggested strategies – adult faith development; ritual re-awakening; ethical responsibility primarily in the hands of government – feel very much like long-term ideal solutions, and to many people will sound totally unrealistic. In times of rapid cultural change, one that probably has evolutionary impetus within it, we must entertain such drastic solutions. We are moving into a new era requiring imagination and creativity as resources, not merely for survival, but for a more meaningful way of living into what is still a largely unknown future.

And the cautious will add: 'OK, but let's slow down the pace, and deal with one challenge at a time.' Personally, I don't think we have much time to spare. The coming years will be a crucial landmark, a crucible that requires of the Island of Saints and Scholars all the creativity we can muster, a departure point that could define our identity – and our spirituality – for many decades thereafter.

Future Vision

The essays in this book aim to depict hope and promise for tomorrow's Ireland. I have tried to honour that goal in the reflections outlined above. So many people, in several countries, have been deluded into following utopian dreams that ended not merely in disappointment but were a disaster for the long-term future. True hope is not born out of false misleading utopias, but out of truth and honesty around the painful issues that need to be encountered, and the painful transitions that need to be negotiated.

Our inherited Christian faith indicates all too clearly that there can be no resurrection without a Calvary preceding it. Through years of persecution, struggle and hope, the Irish church has proclaimed the redemptive power of the paschal journey, centred on the death and resurrection of Jesus. The church itself now needs to become the subject of that same transformative message, realising that on this occasion it is the church itself that will be crucified and the resurrection will happen primarily through the rank-and-file of God's people. And for the people of Ireland, where do we look for guidance and wisdom to embrace this daunting challenge?

In the immediate future, the wisdom of Mother Church is not likely to be of much use. Harkening to the inspiring call of Vatican Two – which the institutional church itself has scarcely honoured – we must now wake up to the fact that we are the church. The faith and hope of future Ireland is in our hands! A grave responsibility indeed, with a challenge that may seem overwhelming. Hopefully, the reflections I offer will at least alert us to what lies ahead. Better still, they may help to inaugurate – and guide – the dialogue and conversation that needs to begin as soon as possible.

References:

Clarke, R. (2007), *A Whisper of God: Essays on Post-Catholic Ireland and the Christian Future*, Dublin: Columba Press.

Flanagan, B. and Kelly D. (2004), *Lamplighters: Exploring Spirituality in New Contexts*, Dublin: Veritas.

Kübler-Ross, E. (1973), *On Death and Dying*, London: Routledge.

Moore, T. (2004), *Dark Nights of the Soul*, London: Piatkus.

O'Doherty, M. (2008), *Empty Pulpits*, Dublin: Gill & Macmillan.

Ó Murchú, D. (2010), *Adult Faith: Growing in Wisdom and Understanding*, Maryknoll, NY: Orbis.

CHAPTER TWELVE

Energy
Local Energy Resilience

Emer Ó Siochrú

Vision for the Future

My vision is to help design, build and operate mid-size multi-energy support systems in every village and neighbourhood in Ireland. These would model socio-ecological complex adaptive systems[1] of the natural world and would add resilience in the face of peak-oil and other shocks by bridging the gap between existing large-scale national systems and the micro-scale household.

Irish-born engineer Mike Cooley famously re-posited Marx's question about what model the economy should adopt, 'The architect or the bee?' in the early 1980s.[2] For Marx and Cooley, the bee did not work but behaved mindlessly by instinct in contrast to humans who should be enabled to work with purpose instead of responding to market signals. Although an inspirational and compassionate writer, Cooley did not understand the honeybee's co-evolution with humans – and so missed what she and the beekeeper could tell us about active management of natural resources and ecosystems for mutual benefit.[3]

I suggest that the question of which model is right is not either/or, but both together; just as the honeybee's purpose and existence is now bound up with ours and ours with hers. My vision sees the humans designing not things but complex adaptive systems like the honeybee hive. These systems can be managed purposefully to serve human needs while still retaining their dynamic self-organisation. Energy is at the heart of all complex adaptive systems, and for the bee it is condensed into nectar and

1. Social-ecological system (SES) – an integrated system of ecosystems and human society with reciprocal feedback and interdependence. The concept emphasises the 'humans-in-nature' perspective.
2. Cooley (1982)
3. De Bruyn (1997)

pollen, the end product of the plant's photosynthesis of solar energy. Human systems are also dependent on solar energy, whether the stored capital of fossil fuels or the solar incomes of sunlight, wind, wave, tides and bio-energy of wood fuels and food. Energy cannot be isolated to a single discrete input but runs through the system taking many different forms. Energy is essential to the functioning of all systems operating at every scale within an integrated whole. Thus the agricultural system, planning system, waste processing, and even the money system are all part of an interlinked energy system.[4]

Clear and Present Danger
The discovery of novel energy sources has shaped human history – starting with wood that burned and cooked food that released higher levels of nutrients for brain development and muscle energy, then the domesticated animals that brought motive power, then water and wind for food and material processing, to the coal that sparked the industrial revolution. In the period between the World Wars, human economic and social development was comprehensively transformed by abundant and cheaply available oil. Oil is an extraordinarily wonderful energy carrier – dense, versatile and easy to store. Nothing else, even gas, quite substitutes. Renewable energy and nuclear energy combined can never completely replace oil in the global economy or in modern urban and rural settlements that have co-evolved to match its particular characteristics.

Many geologists and economists now fear that the increasing scarcity of oil as supplies peak,[5] may trigger a reverse process of global de-development. The shock to oil-dependent infrastructure and systems could be overwhelming because of the nature of our deeply interlinked production and financial systems. Following oil, gas is due to peak within our lifetimes and to do so quite suddenly because of its exploitation characteristics. Into this dangerous scenario comes the even larger and more unpredictable threat of climate change, which will severely constrain

4. Hall *et al* (2003), pp 318-322
5. Peak oil refers to the point at which it will be impossible to maintain a constant output of oil, and supply will level and begin to fall.

our responses to the energy threats as we mitigate and adapt to it.

If these warnings have substance, we must pay attention as the consequences are so serious, and Ireland is in a particularly perilous place. Ireland's energy import dependency was 91% in 2006.[6] In 1990 Irish-based energy production was at 32% of the total but this has reduced to 16% in 2010 as a result of the increase in consumption and the decrease in domestic production of Kinsale gas.[7] Most Irish fossil energy imports comprise oil from the UK and Norway and natural gas from the UK, all of which are nearing depletion. As a result we are hugely vulnerable to the political and market instabilities of fossil energy exporters.

The existing grid system and electricity industry globally is in the midst of profound and comprehensive change, including a return to the local and neighbourhood scale in which the industry's early history is rooted. As Amory B. Lovins[8] points out, the grid linking central stations to remote customers has become the main driver of power-quality problems. The cheapest, most reliable power, therefore, is now electricity produced at or near the customers. However, Irish government energy policy is currently geared to the national scale. Electricity is generated in a few large plants at a distance from where it is consumed and the electricity transmission grid is completely separate from the distribution grid. The government, under EU direction, is making plans to introduce competition in energy generation and services. I believe that there are serious risks in replacing public ownership of energy assets with private ownership while retaining the current centralised structure and linear processes.

There is a direct relation between connectedness and rigidity that leads to vulnerability and fragility and thus unexpected collapse. An energy crisis would be considerably worse for Irish citizens than the banking crisis as the solutions would not lie in new monetary policies and financial regulation (which the government did not adopt, unfortunately), but in the laws of physics that are beyond the reach of democratic persuasion.

6. Rourke *et al* (2009), pp 1975-1984
7. Bazilian *et al* (2006)
8. Lovins *et al* (2006)

Formula for Energy Resilience

Although recovery from an energy shock would be extraordinarily difficult as it would require energy to muster emergency responses and reconstruction, preparation before oil-peak yields high benefits to first movers.[9] If we move quickly before supplies are constrained and before other nation states race to secure fossil fuel supplies and thus raise prices, we can considerably improve the quality of our post-peak lives. Within this perspective, the global economic downturn that has depressed oil demand to $80 a barrel is an opportunity not to be missed.

Secondly, the laws of physics – so threatening when we ignore them – point to a mechanism that can leverage our actions in the short space of time we have left to build resilience to energy shocks and shortage. Resilience[10] is defined as the capacity of a system to absorb disturbance and reorganise while undergoing change so as to retain essentially the same function, structure identity and feedbacks; that is, to remain within one regime. In this context 'regime change' is generally not a good thing! Natural science has uncovered universal laws governing physical systems at every scale from the microscopic to galaxies. These laws can also be observed in human social and economic systems and critically in systems that include both humans and environmental systems in interaction.[11] It appears that at least in this respect, humans are fully part and parcel of the natural world!

The actively managed 'wild' honeybee hive is a very resilient and productive enterprise – much more productive than fully domesticated animal husbandry systems that require considerable farmer, machine and energy input. The good beekeeper is the conscious ruler of the managed hive; noting nectar and pollen supplies, egg production, drone and queen cells and signs of disease, all in the context of weather and plant bloom forecasts. She intervenes at the optimal part of the cycle by feeding, removing cells, moving frames and creating new hive nuclei; all to get the best outcome for bees and humans alike. This can be described as a 'social-ecological system' where the

9. Korowicz (2010)
10. Walker *et al* (2004)
11. Norberg *et al* (2008)

natural reactive and autonomous feedbacks system of the honey-bees is replaced by proactive human capacity for information processing, planning and foresight. The time input by the bee-keeper is no more than 20 minutes a week for two months of the year. The bees still do most of the work to produce in an average year 50lbs of honey or a good hive in an exceptional year up to 300lbs of honey. Wax is also produced, worth in some cases more than the honey for use in pharmaceuticals. But the pollin-ation work is almost priceless. It was estimated that the honey-bee's pollination services were worth $16 billion annually in the US in 1997 alone.[12] This is the factor of return on energy invest-ment (EROEI)[13] we should aim for in a new energy system for Ireland.

The task then is to augment our single centralised and linear energy, food, planning and financial systems with a new set of consciously-designed complex adaptive systems at local level providing similar services but at a much lower resource input level.[14] More food, fuel, and fibre will have to be coaxed from nature while high ecosystem values and services are sustained. In short, to build resilience we must become 'keepers' of local in-tegrated life support systems attuned to the wider environment.

Scale and Diversity

The scale appropriate for active management of complex sys-tems is one where all the main elements of a life support system are in place so that learning by experimentation is possible.[15] There are particular benefits to acting on the local or mid scale – the size of the local ecosystem and local governance unit.[16] The village, small town or neighbourhood of 60-1000 homes can en-compass all the basic elements for immediate human subsist-ence of water, food, shelter, warmth, transport and social and cultural supports. All these systems interact poorly in a linear

---

12. Pimentel *et al* (1997), pp 747–757
13. The EROEI is the ratio of the energy that is produced to all the energy used to discover and produce that energy. See: Prof C. Hall, http://www.feasta.org/events/general/hall_lecture.
14. Day *et al* (2009), p 328
15. Gunderson and Holling (2002)
16. Norberg *et al* (2008)

mechanistic manner at the moment but they are capable, at this scale, of transformation into a managed adaptive system. People can comprehend a subset of the real world, i.e. a lower-dimensional representation of the whole because that is where they immediately experience it.[17] Proactive design and management of the system at this local scale will dampen shocks rippling through the national system and buy time to reorganise.

Experiencing dynamic change in small systems and going through the process of recovery/restructuring can prevent the unrecoverable collapse of the entire system. For example, the forestry policy that suppressed forest fires in the US created the conditions for the eventual conflagration of the entire forest because of the resulting build-up of dry undergrowth which was far more devastating to wildlife and plant regeneration than a series of smaller fires. This led to a change in forestry policy to allow and manage local forest fires.

Single isolated homes are particularly vulnerable to oil-peak and to severe climate events as we saw in the severe winter of 2009-10. The lifestyle choice to live in the open countryside and commute to work is an example of cultural adaptation to the cheap oil era that is coming to an end. The costs of maintaining roads and servicing families living in scattered dwellings will drain resources from settlements where the same investment would give much greater social, economic and environmental returns. No level of micro-renewable energy investment or passive-house design can offset the resilience of a well-managed local support system.[18] Whether in urban or rural areas, investment in energy efficiency and micro generation at single household level will not give the same returns as the same investment in grouped systems.

Diversity is important too. Ecologists have noted that during reorganisation after disturbances the potential for input of a diversity of species directly determines the rate at which the system may self-organise toward a community that reflects local conditions.[19] Policies based on general themes often fail because they miss important details of local conditions – context is im-

17. Andereis and Norberg (2008)
18. Ó Siochrú (forthcoming, 2010)
19. Ibid

portant. Multiple stakeholder participation is another way to minimise the dominance of single solutions.

What this means for us is that the more and different local energy solutions there are, the quicker the recovery following disturbance, as amongst them will surely be some that work particularly well or that are particularly robust and these can be quickly copied. The benefits of community scale generation are already evident in other European countries. Gussing, a small town in Austria, has a rape-oil-refinery that produces biodiesel, a district heating unit supplied with wood, and a state of the art biomass-power plant that generates 2 MW electricity and 4.5 MW heat. The town is 45% self sufficient in energy. It has attracted 50 new companies, more than 1,000 new jobs, and a total increased sales volume of 13m Euro/year. Lunen is another example of community scale generation. It uses organic material from local farms to provide electricity for its 90,000 residents. The plant produces 6.8 MW of power from the organic waste. This provides heat for 26,000 houses. The biomethane gas is distributed through an underground biogas pipeline network.

Synergies and Bio-energy
A new energy system for Ireland should look for and design for 'complementarities' or 'synergies'. Technologies that can use local waste, i.e. the output of one process or species, as the input for another are particularly useful. This is where bio-energy technologies win over wind and wave technologies that make electricity only.

Anaerobic digestion of organic biomass and agricultural and other food wastes is the most complementary energy technology available in Ireland at this time and thus the most immediately useful to build resilience. Anaerobic digesters (ADs) can deliver reliable renewable energy for electricity, transport and heat, at a scale where all the energy can be utilised without needing significant new infrastructure. Biomethane is upgraded biogas produced from anaerobic digestion. Ireland has ample food waste, slaughterhouse waste and surplus grass to supply up to 15 PJ (360 ktoe) of energy from biomethane.[20] Biomethane produced

---

20. Singh (2010), pp 277-288

from grass requires one third of the land required for ethanol production and one eighteenth of the land required for rapeseed biodiesel. It is by far the most efficient means of producing transport fuel from Irish farmland.[21] As transport energy accounts for 42% of total Irish energy use it will be the sector hardest hit by oil peak, as it is almost completely oil dependent. Petrol vehicles can be altered relatively easily to run on biomethane. Biomethane can also be injected into the natural gas grid and used in existing heating and cooking appliances with a little modification.

These facts alone should make the widespread development of anaerobic digestion of organic material a priority for emergency planning under the National Renewable Energy Action Plan (NREAP).

Anaerobic digesters reduce nitrates pollution in water, the need for artificial fertilisers and thus the level of nitrous oxide emissions from the soil. Finally, considerable quantities of methane emissions are avoided when manure is digested properly rather than stored as slurry.

Cities and towns generate considerable food, sewage and other biological wastes that can no longer be landfilled or spread under the EU Landfill Directive. The 'gate fees' (fees charged to process this biodegradable waste) will be substantial for some years to come – circa €60-100 per ton. The co-digestion of food waste with manure produces a much more stable AD process than when food waste is processed as a sole feedstock. The income from gate fees and the reduction in farm production costs resulting from using digestate from anaerobic digestion instead of buying fertilisers can add considerably to farm incomes at a time when it is sorely needed.

Putting it all Together

We have now most of the ingredients of a managed complex adaptive system of our formula for energy resilience in rural areas. The formula requires one further input which transforms the economic and environmental equation to multiply return on capital. That element is human waste. Conventional human

---

21. Murphy (2009), pp 504-512

waste processing is egregiously wasteful of water, energy and nutrients: a fact that has received little critical attention from environmentalists although sewage pollutants in ground water are well recognised. Anaerobic digestion is already used to process the sludge from conventional sewage plants into a stable soil amendment. The question arises then, why not pipe fresh sewage directly into an AD and bypass the expensive and not very effective 'water treatment' plant? The obstacle is the high volume of water needed to transport waste in gravity drainage systems and the fact that anaerobic digesters cannot operate efficiently with very high water content. The answer is over-looked Victorian technologies – vacuum sewers – that require very little water to transport waste.

Vacuum technology is based on differential air pressure and drainage, making it cheaper to build and install than conventional systems. When a system is well designed, the sewers have ab-solutely no leakages (vacuum avoids exfiltration) so sewers may be laid in the same trench as other mains including potable water or rain-water and in water protection areas.

Although the energy and environmental benefits of rural anaerobic digesters processing human, food and agricultural wastes together are convincing, the financial argument for them is overwhelming. For the same cost or less (circa €1.7 million) of a conventional 'wastewater' treatment plant that will cost a fur-ther €40,000 *per annum* to maintain, a village could build an anaerobic digester with combined heat and power plant which would not only pay for its construction and running costs but produce an annual surplus to satisfy investors. It would com-prise a resilient life support system for the community, one that protects existing bio-system services, recycles wastes to increase agricultural productivity, and provides energy in four different forms not counting food.

The addition of a managed private wire serving the area would facilitate renewable energy production from wind, as electricity generation from biogas can alter output to maintain a steady current whatever the weather. With local energy grids come the potential to manage energy demand with smart grid and meter technologies. The electrical generation capacity re-quired in a managed embedded energy system is approximately

2/3rds that required for a conventional grid system.[22] A balanced land-use plan is the best foundation for such technology – yet another good reason to build settlements with living, working and service areas in close proximity.

Social sustainability dictates that the economic returns of the system do not flow to an elite few but to a wide group, especially the farmers who maintain environmental services and produce the food. Farmers have a strong claim to urban food waste on advantageous terms, as without the return of a significant percentage of the original agricultural production of the land, to the land, the nutrient cycle cannot be closed.

Other Potential Systems
Closing nutrient and energy loops by anaerobic digestion is but one example of a viable managed complex adaptive system. It suits locations with good agricultural land, a large number of housed animals within 5km, food waste within 20km and a requirement to upgrade sewage treatment facilities within 1km. These conditions are met in large areas of the midlands and south west of Ireland. For poorer land in more mountainous areas, a different configuration of feedstocks and technology that builds on its unique ecosystem services and agricultural production characteristics is mandated. A good candidate is one centred on the pyrolysis of woody biomass wastes and biomass crops to produce a variety of useful energy products and services. Pyrolysis suits upland forested areas found mainly in the West where it is difficult to make a decent income from farming alone.

If our aim is to rapidly build local resilience by producing energy and food while enhancing ecosystem services, easily the most exciting product of pyrolysis reactors is biochar. Biochar is produced from the biomass that has taken up CO_2 in its growing phase in such a way that 25%-50% of the CO_2 is locked into the char as carbon. When applied to the soil the biochar contributes its own stable carbon and stimulates further CO_2/carbon uptake and storage by soil microbes.[23] Applied to poor or degraded

22. Ó Siochrú *et al* (2004)
23. Kwapinski *et al* (2010)

soils, biochar has shown very significant increases in crop yields as well as reduced nitrous oxide (a powerful greenhouse gas) emissions from the soil. These attributes make pyrolysis for biochar one of the very few technologies powerful enough to address the climate change challenge without reducing food security as attested by James Hansen.[24]

There is a great deal still to be learnt about the exact processing conditions to manufacture biochar to give predictable results so that it can be sold as a high valuable soil amendment, i.e. higher value than the energy content of the char. Biochar is not a new discovery. The ancient Amazonians created the *Terra Preta* ('dark earth' in Portuguese), extraordinarily productive soils that fed a sophisticated civilisation[25] for hundreds of years before the *conquistadores* brought the diseases that ended it abruptly. Unfortunately, there are things that the ancients knew which must be re-discovered before modern biochar can match the amazing productivity and renewability of *Terra Preta*.

Luckily for us, Ireland has one of the leading biochar/Terra Preta research centres in the world based in University of Limerick and headed by Dr Michael Hayes.[26] Their research and crop trials are indicating promising results. With modest government support we can be reasonably confident that the last piece of the biochar puzzle will soon be in place to balance the economic equation.

Challenges

Accommodating large-scale wind developers in the current government's plans for renewable energy in the National Renewable Energy Action Plan (NREAP) will divert resources and starve investment from smaller scale embedded energy generation that does not have the same requirements for comprehensive grid upgrade. The drive to optimise efficiency leads to the exploitation of the best terrestrial wind sites that are invariably in remote areas, often with high biodiversity value.

---

24. Hansen *et al* (in press)
25. Sombroek *et al* (2003), pp 125-139
26. Carbolea, *Advanced Biomass Research for Beyond the Petroleum Age*, See: http://www.carbolea.ul.ie/biochar

Some of the proposed wind farms that have planning permission and connection offers are in areas now designated as Natura 2000 sites with vulnerable bird migration patterns or in upland peat-bogs whose valuable carbon storage systems will be compromised. While large-scale wind projects, perhaps offshore and/or perhaps combined with hydro-storage do have potential, resilience cannot be built at the cost of biodiversity or a stable climate.

Policy makers seem oblivious to the potential of mid-scale renewables and of local authorities to find synergies and lead the transition to a low carbon future. Mid-size local renewable energy generation is greatly facilitated by access to a 'private wire' – the electrical infrastructure necessary to supply electricity directly to third parties located near the generator, independent of the national transmission/distribution system. But the NREAP is unenthusiastic. It notes a provision under Directive 2009/72/EC that owners of a private network must allow full third party access for alternative suppliers through its network. This means mid-size electricity producers must sell their electricity into the monopoly that is ESB Networks, owned and operated by the ESB, the dominant energy supplier, and cannot use long-term purchase agreements with customers to help fund their initial investment. Or as one frustrated mid-size renewable developer put it, 'it's like selling bread to a baker.'

In short, the NREAP as it stands does not recognise mid-size generation as an essential element of Irish energy resilience, does not recognise the multi-benefits of bio-energy, provides no assistance with 'private wire' and gives no particular role to local authorities in the development of energy resilience.

The financial crisis may be our best ally in getting a change of course as the economic benefits of the distributed, embedded bio-energy model, especially for anaerobic digestion, are so compelling. Even one demonstration project would be very persuasive.

There are further serious threats to mid-scale bio-energy projects. Many large urban-based anaerobic digesters are in the planning pipeline and have been attracted by the super profit potential of gate fees introduced under new regulations to reduce landfill. Their focus will be on the gate fee and electricity generation revenue and not on producing useful fertiliser or ecosystem services. With maximising throughput comes increased risk that the digested material might not be fully digested (stabilised) and therefore not be of any use in agriculture. Nevertheless, mega anaerobic digesters promoted by waste companies who have regulated monopolies of municipal waste could crowd out mid-scale projects set in rural areas. The same dynamics may prevent the adoption of pyrolysis systems delivering integrated solutions at local level.

Gate fees and tariffs must be carefully set and adjusted to foster the more resilience-building solutions. Planners, Services Engineers and County Managers should be alive to assisting mid-size local initiatives and not conflate them with the large waste-processing projects that are more of a burden than an asset to a local community.

Another obstacle to this energy vision relates to landownership patterns and privileges. A managed complex adaptive energy system, bringing many local benefits, will add value to nearby land that can connect to it. The landowners of such land who have not have made any contribution to the project can pocket this added value through a higher sale price or higher rents. The project developer can get income through the sale of electricity, heat and gas to locals but cannot recoup any of this 'connectivity' value on 3rd party land. Neither can the local authority, which may be a partner in the project, recoup a share of the value created, under its current powers.

A Site Value Tax (SVT) could transform this situation by capturing some of this upswing in value for re-investment in further resilience building projects. It would enable local authorities to lead development of managed complex adaptive energy systems because they could be partly financed from site value tax income. It is of utmost importance therefore that the proposal for a Site Value Tax in the current Programme for Government comes to fruition. A Site Value Tax will dampen incentives to speculate in property in the hopes of reaping unearned gains through general economic uplift – the end game of which has nearly destroyed the economy. This should liberate savings for investment in truly productive assets and there are none better than renewable energy. Widespread ownership of mid-size embedded energy assets should be actively fostered with new company structures and partnerships between developers, farmers, and consumers backed up by tax incentives aimed at pension funds and ordinary people.

Finally, a multi-disciplinary approach is needed to build successful social-ecological systems. It is time to ditch blinkered, over-specialised professions and departments. The integration of architectural and structural, energy and sanitary engineering, farming, ecological and financial expertise is needed to replace the current practice of designing and managing naturally interacting elements in isolation. Although necessarily complicated because of the synergistic functioning, the technology should not be complex, i.e. it should be sufficiently simple and robust that local expertise can fix any problem that might arise. The benefits to community-run energy systems are local expertise, local job creation and community resilience.

Postscript

It is ironic to note that as the Congested Districts Board was busy scattering the village settlements along the West coast at the end of the 19th century and resettling the people in isolated farm holdings (thus setting the seeds of emigration for years to come), it also distributed specially designed beehives to the hapless farmers. The CDB hive as it was known, was manufactured and sold by Abbott Bros in Dublin and is still used in windy and wet locations throughout these islands. Hardy Irish black bees were also distributed to the farmsteads where they thrived until farming practices changed. Despite modernisation, 60% of honeybees in Ireland survived in the wild until the turn of the millennium when they were all but wiped out by the Varroa mite that was carelessly, if not criminally imported with a consignment of non-native bees. The Irish bee did survive; some in the mountains and some in the midland bogs were adopted by an unsung Irish hero, Jim Donohue of the *Midland Beekeepers Association*.[27] Jim has been breeding to improve temper and productivity of the bog bee at his base in Belvedere House, Mullingar for over

27. Midlands Beekeepers Association, Belvedere House and Gardens, Mullingar. See http://www.irishbeekeeping.ie/federation/affassoc-txt.html#midlands

20 years. He has developed a system that manages hives so well that he can produce 40 new healthy, gentle colonies a year. He trains new beekeepers to replicate his results in order to create an abundance of healthy bee colonies ideally suited to Irish conditions that can survive any external or internal threat.

That should be our aim too.

References:

Andereis, J. and Norberg, J. (2008), 'Theoretical Challenges', in Norberg, J. and Cumming G. S., eds. *Complexity Theory for a Sustainable Future*, New York: Columbia University Press.

Bazilian, M., O'Leary, F., O'Gallagher, B., and Howley, M. (2006), *Security of Supply in Ireland*, SEI.

Cooley, M. (1982), *Architect Or Bee? The Human/Technology Relationship*, Boston: South End Press.

Day, J. W. *et al* (2009), Ecology in Times of Scarcity, *BioScience* 59 (4).

De Bruyn, C. (1997), *Practical Beekeeping*, Crowood Press.

Gunderson, L. H., and Holling, C. S. (2002), *Panarchy – Understanding transformations in human and natural systems*, Island Press.

Hall, C. *et al* (2003), Hydrocarbons and the evolution of human culture, *Nature* 426.

Hansen, J. *et al* (In press) 'Target Atmospheric CO_2: Where Should Humanity Aim?' [Supporting materials].

Korowicz, D. (2010), *Tipping Point*, Available from: http://www.feasta.org.

Kwapinski, W. *et al* (2010), Biochar from biomass and waste, *Waste and Biomass Valorization Journal*, DOI 10.1007/s12649-010-9024-8

Lovins, A. B., Datta, E. K., Feiler, T., Lehmann, A., Rabago, K. R., Swisher, J. N. and Wiker, K., (2006), *Small is Profitable: The Hidden Economic Benefits of Making Electrical Resources the Right Size*, Rocky Mountain Institute.

Midlands Beekeepers Association, Belvedere House and Gardens, Mullingar. See: http://www.irishbeekeeping.ie/federation/affassoctxt.html#midlands

Murphy, J. D. (2009), An argument for using biomethane generated from grass as a biofuel in Ireland, *Biomass and Bioenergy* 33.

Norberg, J., Wilson, J., Walker, B. and Ostrom, E. (2008), 'Diversity and Resilience of Social-ecological systems' in Norberg, J. and Cumming, G.S., eds, *Complexity Theory for a Sustainable Future*, New York: Columbia University Press.

Ó Siochrú, E. *et al* (2004), *ENLIVEN Report*, Irish Rural Link & Feasta. Available from: http://www.feasta.org

Ó Siochrú, E. (forthcoming publication 2010) *Proximity 2.0, The New Emergency*, Feasta.

Pimentel, D. (1997), Economic and environmental benefits of biodiversity, *BioScience* 47 (11).

Rourke, F., Boyle, F. and Reynolds, A. (2009), Renewable energy resources and technologies applicable to Ireland, *Renewable and Sustainable Energy Reviews* 13 (8).

Singh, A. (2010), A Biofuel Strategy for Ireland with an emphasis on production of biomethane and minimisation of land-take, *Renewable and Sustainable Energy Reviews* 14 (1).

Sombroek, W. *et al* (2003), 'Amazonian Dark Earths as carbon stores and sinks' in Lehmann, J. K. et al, eds, *Amazonian Dark Earths: Origin, Properties, Management*, Dordrecht: Kluwer Academic Publishers.

Tainter, J. (1988), The Collapse of Complex Societies, *New Studies in Archaeology*, Cambridge University Press.

Walker, B. *et al* (2004), Resilience Adaptability and Transformability in Social-Ecological systems, *Ecology and Society* 9 (2): 5. Available from http://www.ecologyandsociety.org/vol19/1222/art5

CHAPTER THIRTEEN

Farming and Food
A New Future for Farming

John Feehan

We find it difficult for all sorts of reasons to see more than a decade into the future. Back in 1950 could we ever have imagined what the world of 2010 would be like? Global warming and the biodiversity crisis did not exist for us then, nor was there any awareness of the population explosion or the global water crisis we are now faced with, or the challenge of feeding 9 billion in a water-challenged world. All of our attention was on the task of coaxing into flame the glowing embers of an economy that had very few natural resources at its disposal.

Feeding a world of 9 billion people
It is expected that the human population of the earth will peak at some 9 billion by 2050, two-thirds of whom will be in dense conurbations to which they have moved because they can no longer find enough to support them in the countryside. These people will not have the land resources to feed themselves, and will depend increasingly not on food produced in the urban hinterland or indeed elsewhere in their own country, but on imported food. Globally, there is no more land. All the good land is already in production. Most of what is left is desert, mountain or city: and indeed, in 2006 the International Food Policy Research Institute reported that 40 per cent of what is farmed today is seriously degraded. We cannot afford to lose any more farmland: we will need every hectare of agricultural land we have.

Already countries that are experiencing this urban population explosion depend to a large extent on imported food. The inevitable rise in the price of grain tracking the rise in the price of oil makes it more expensive for these countries to import what they need to feed their people. Worldwide, 95 per cent of all food production depends on oil; around a third of this goes to make artificial fertilisers, a further third to power agricultural

machinery, and the remaining third is used for irrigation, pesticides and so on. In 2008 there were food riots in Egypt, Haiti and
El Salvador. This is likely to become the norm in the decades to
come.

Here in Ireland we are in a privileged position. We will have
ample supplies of water into the foreseeable future, and the
marginal land allowed to slip out of productive agriculture constitutes a productive land bank that can be reclaimed. We will
see farmed once more land on the margins that was taken into
production in earlier times and abandoned as the tide of
intensification concentrated on the 'best' land: not the extensive
acres on the hills taken from the wild as the population rose to
its pre-Famine peak of eight million people to be fed from local
resources: but the countless acres that lie fallow in small pockets
everywhere: individually small, but cumulatively of great extent, in town as well as in the countryside.

This land cannot be made productive, however, by applying
the oil-dependent intensive techniques of the last 60 years,
which will have become obsolete half a century hence. In a future
in which the high price of oil will have made the extensive use of
fertiliser uneconomic, we will need to develop – or recover – an
agriculture that is based on inherent fertility. This will require
an understanding not only of the principles of the applied science of agro-ecology, but of how those principles are to be applied in the unique circumstances of each place. In its newfound
adherence to the principles of self-sufficiency, this new agriculture will be a return to the older knowledge of the past, but the
greater understanding and control which the advance of science
and technology have given us will mean that it is enhanced by
the best of appropriate technology.

Towards a farming independent of oil
The farm of the future cannot afford the extravagant waste involved in excessive fertiliser use. It cannot afford it in the first
place because it is too costly. It is too costly also in terms of the
price paid for its use in other areas. As far back as the middle of
the 19th century, when progressive farmers were beginning to
make use of guano imported from South America, Edmund
Murphy commented on the way 'we send to our Antipodes for

the very manure which, to an almost unlimited extent, we suffer to pollute our rivers, rendering their waters unwholesome, and to be by them deposited in the depths of the ocean.'[1] The cost of remedying the pollution of water and soil is part of the true cost of relying on external inputs for fertility. Add to all of this the price paid in terms of loss of natural habitat and of biodiversity throughout Europe, but especially in those parts of Europe where farming has been most mechanised in order to make optimal use of the saving in manpower and labour costs made possible by technological development: itself dependent on the use of fossil fuels to substitute for the use of human and animal muscle power.

All of this runs directly counter to a way of farming which sought to maximise fertility and production through the optimal use of internal, local resources and which was reaching a considerable level of skill in doing so by the early 20th century. Intelligent practical farmers and their agricultural advisors had developed great skill and understanding of the maintenance of fertility through management of a mixed sward that varied in composition for different kinds of farming under different sets of geographical circumstances, using only internal sources of compost and manure. The establishment of the Department of Agriculture and Technical Instruction for Ireland at the end of the 19th century provided the opportunity to promulgate the new skills among the new yeoman farmers of Ireland, but was insufficiently resourced to have much impact outside the immediate circle of influence of those trained by it. The rise of the new mode of farming, whose costs we are grappling with today, was not due to any inherent superiority in terms of its productivity, but the result of the inappropriate influence of vested economic interest of the industries that had most to gain from unlimited use of fossil fuel and fertiliser.[2]

Another unforeseen cost is the effect of the clover-ryegrass diet on animal health and welfare. The superior quality of the ryegrass sward on the best soils had long been recognised – with reservations – but the animals' diet was not restricted to it. The

1. Murphy (1846)
2. Feehan (2003)

mixed sward of High Farming[3] provided grazing animals with a nutritionally varied and balanced diet conducive to better health and greater contentment. Today we are concerned in an unprecedented way with animal welfare, and methods of animal husbandry conducive to better welfare are more likely to win favour with the buying public and can be exploited by the farmer to help offset any immediate decrease in income that results from losses of 'productivity' resulting from the adoption of more extensive methods. Reduced veterinary bills, and the greater satisfaction that accompanies the work of developing the new skills required are all factors that further restore the balance.

The problems associated with the breeding of animals purely for yield as estimated by weight and monetary outcome are being recognised increasingly. The new paradigm for sustainable agriculture currently being modeled by Liam Downey and Gordon Purvis at UCD has as one of its two poles *rumen function*: in effect, a farm on which the animals are healthy and happy as well as productive. The other pole is pasture management that provides this while at the same time maintaining biodiversity, landscape quality and the physical and chemical integrity of air, soil and water.[4]

We can recover the understanding and practical skills required to implement such a model, but it will not be easy. Our adoption of it may be reluctant, but in the medium to long term it will be imposed by global population, resource depletion and general economic trends. It will require a new way of thinking about the level of education required for farmers to acquire this level of understanding and skill: but before that it is important for farmers to see what is possible: to see all that might be recovered by such change of direction.

Urban agriculture
Urban agriculture will also be part of the answer everywhere. Currently 800 million people are already involved worldwide,

3. This refers to the heyday of the 'convertible agriculture' that underpinned the Agricultural Revolution (i.e. the incorporation of grass-legume mixtures in rotations in order to maintain fertility).
4. Purvis *et al* (in prep.)

and not only in developing countries. In the late 1990s one in ten families in some US cities were engaged in urban farming, and in Moscow two-thirds of families. In mid-19th century Paris one-sixth of the city was farmed (using the abundant horse manure available in those days): it was self-sufficient in greens, fruits and vegetables.

A new farming paradigm
To get where we need to be requires enlightened agriculture. The future will need good farmers and lots of them. That requires real skill and the experience of generations, using the best of science and appropriate technology (geared to the small, mixed farm): and it needs hands as well as brains. It cannot be practised by one farmer on a thousand hectares, which is the ambition today. Enlightened agriculture is mixed and small-scale, combining the accumulated agronomic wisdom of millennia with the best of scientific understanding. It would provide the best and freshest possible food and lead to national self-reliance worldwide, while trading abroad only those commodities they have in excess and for which they have guaranteed markets. If countries such as Angola and Ethiopia – even – had new agrarian economies geared to their own local variety of enlightened agriculture they could be self-reliant on food several times over. And it needs agrarian communities to support them.[5]

We need a new agricultural model, a new farming philosophy. We need another agricultural revolution: an agrarian economy that is based on local adaptation of economic activity to the capacity of the land to sustain such activity. Farming with brains rather than by habit or convenience: to merge traditional knowledge and experience with modern understanding of ecology in order to sustain agriculture in a way that can feed the population of the 21st century. Many of the simple steps that lead to such a new model are already part and parcel of organic farming: the conservation and use of manure that can increase the abundance of earthworms and soil micro-organisms five-fold, or of the straw mulching that can triple the mass of the soil biota. In an extraordinary series of experiments carried on at

5. Feehan (2003)

Rothamsted between 1845 and 1975 plots treated with farmyard manure for more than a hundred years nearly tripled in soil nitrogen content whereas nearly all the nitrogen added in chemical fertiliser was lost to the soil – either exported in crops or dissolved in runoff.

This new farming paradigm will see farming as the skilled profession it needs to be – as a vocation even – that like other esteemed professions will be able to retain its share of the best minds and hearts in society. This will also require us to restore a system of farmer education that is adequate to this challenge: far removed from that which has come to be considered adequate in our time. Agricultural education for the new future will require not only the re-establishment of a properly holistic agricultural education for those who work in an advisory capacity, but of farmer education at this level. The emphasis in agricultural education from its auspicious beginnings in the late 19th century was on the training of advisors and instructors in agriculture rather than farmers. This needs to be changed, so that the intake at third level in agriculture is dominated by the men and women who actually farm the land: just as a medical faculty is dominated by trainee doctors who will actually treat the sick, not those who advise and sell to them.

The future of Ireland's bogs

Sixty years ago we could not have foreseen that we would come to value the other functions of nature in a way that might in certain circumstances outweigh what in conventional economics would be considered the more obviously productive functions. We understand and appreciate much better than we did 50 or 60 years ago the many ecosystem services other than production (in the narrow economic sense) that different dimensions and facets of natural ecosystems perform in our lives. In the economy of the Midlands in the decades following the establishment of Bord na Móna in 1946, for instance, the bogs were of greatest value to us as a source of the raw material from which we could make turf or briquettes, or burn to generate electricity. We had little time or leisure to consider the recreational, aesthetic, ecological, cultural or spiritual functions they served.[6]

6. Feehan (2008)

A few decades from now the great machines will fall silent, and take their place in the iron graveyards and museums where earlier models already rust. We will still be here then, when there is no more turf to burn. Our children will be here in 50 years, when oil will be too precious to burn. By that time there will be concern over the ecological change consequent on global warming in those bogs on which we have conferred a conservation status equivalent to 'hotspots.' The most recent analysis warns us of the possibility that unharvested peatlands may even be eliminated by climatic change predicted for the rest of this century.[7]

And although we cannot see into the future, and our capacity to imagine what the future might be like is limited by the conditioning of our psychological heritage, we can discern the challenge that reaches back to us from that future half a century and further hence, when the inevitable trends we can read today in human population growth and world farming will have compelled us into a new self-sufficiency we might have adopted with less pain if we humans had greater capacity and determination to use our knowledge and insight to plan for a time fifty years down the line.

By this time land that we have taken out of production or allowed to decline in productive capacity will need to be reclaimed for a new kind of agriculture: in which new insights of ecology and genetics, and new technologies to facilitate sustainable land management, will be spliced with the techniques of maintaining inherent productivity learned during the several hundred years before they were consigned to a top shelf by the input-intensive model that has dominated the last short 50 years.

The long-term prospect for farming is intimately bound up with the long-term prospect for forestry and peatlands. Fifty years hence we may come to depend much more upon timber for household fuel from the woods now taking hold on much marginal farmland. It is likely that our forest management skills and the energy efficiency measures with which the new woodland resource is managed will by then have come of age, and in

7. Jones *et al* (2006), pp 323-334

parallel with those developments we will see a continuing shift in the balance of the values we set on bogland. There are moves afoot today to move the focus of conservation away from the 'hotspot' approach favoured in recent decades, in which most of our care and resources are targeted on a small number of areas selected on the basis of conservation parameters alone, and to broaden the focus to include all the ecosystem services biological diversity performs for our welfare, and on the economic quantification of these services.

In the changed circumstances of 50 years time it might appear that the afforestation of substantial areas of cutaway bog to supplement planting on more marginal farmland would acquire a new urgency. But even if we assume that continued research can overcome the silvicultural challenges that have hitherto balked economic forestry on cutaway bog, we also need to remember that in the warmer world to come, with a world population of around 9 billion, with biodiversity reduced and confined as never before at a time when we will have come to appreciate as never before the full spectrum of functions it serves in human life, cutaway bog will be treasured as the last place on our doorstep to which we can retreat from our frenetic world in order to experience contact with nature.

While we still await even a preliminary attempt at the economic quantification of ecosystem functions and services in relation to the future of cutaway, it is very clear from comparable studies that their total value to society, to the community, greatly outstrips the purely monetary return to be made by concentrating on any short-term profit.[8] It is short-sighted folly to be experimenting with the planting of energy crops on cutaway bog when there is so much marginal and neglected farmland. There is greater value to society in the long term in facilitating its capacity to fulfill the other ecosystem functions it performs, functions that productive land can less richly perform. We need to concern ourselves now with this perspective if we are to ensure that we don't do something else on our watch that our grandchildren will have cause to blame us for.

All of this will require a cascade of change, a veritable paradigm

---

8. Costanza (1997); European Commission (2008)

shift. It is not something we will implement willingly: we are too enslaved to the comforts of the way we live for that. It is not something we will embrace because reason and moral sensibility have convinced us of its necessity. It will be forced upon us by the unintended consequences of our actions. Nor will it happen overnight, although any one of a hundred possible catastrophic possibilities may hasten its development.

Serendipity in the face of possible catastrophe
The dismay and disruption caused by the recent minor eruption of Eyjafjallajökull show how little it takes to derail our modern way of life, so dependent has it become on increasingly sophisticated technology. With our reliance on globalised trade and food distribution, and on space communication, the most immediate effect of a more geologically significant volcanic event would be on food supply. A report by the Geological Society of London in 2005 soberly concluded that a super-eruption would devastate an area the size of North America or Europe, 'and pronounced deterioration of global climate would be expected for a few years following the eruption. Such events could result in the ruin of world agriculture, severe disruption of food supplies, and mass starvation. The effects could be sufficiently severe to threaten the fabric of civilisation.'

While not imminent, such upheavals are not exceptional – except when measured by the yardstick of human experience. They are a normal and inevitable part of the way the earth works.[9]

Conclusion
History demonstrates our limited success in using our intelligence to foresee and shape our own future. When the great German philosopher Hegel cast his brilliant, encyclopedic mind over the course of human history in the early 19th century, one of the things that struck him above all was that (as he wrote in the introduction to his magisterial *Philosophy of History*) 'What experience and history teach is this – that people and government never have learned anything from history, or acted upon principles deduced from it.' As we try to peer prophetically through the misty curtain of time that stretches in front of us as

9. Sparks and Self (2005)

we attempt to see into the future, we need to remind ourselves how poorly we saw ahead – to the present time – 60 years ago. But at the same time our capacity to see ahead has never been greater, so we should be able to penetrate that temporal mist to some extent: as we need to do if we are to take the right actions now in order to ensure that we do not compromise the future we bequeath to our grandchildren.

References:

Brown, L. (2009), *Plan B 4.0: Mobilizing to Save Civilization*, W. W. Norton & Co.

Costanza, R., Cumberland, J., Daly, H., Goodland, R., and Norgaard, R. (1997), *An Introduction to Ecological Economics*, St Lucie, International Society for Ecological Economics.

European Commission (2008), *The Economics of Ecosystems and Biodiversity report*. Available from http://ec.europa.eu/environment/nature/biodiversity/economics/index_en.htm.

Feehan, J. (2003), *Farming in Ireland: History, Heritage and Environment*, UCD Faculty of Agriculture.

Feehan, J. (2008), *A distant landscape dimly seen: the bogs in 2050*, Proceedings of the 13th International Peat Congress, Tullamore (invited paper). International Peat Society.

Hegel, G. W. F. (1837), *The Philosophy of History*, translated by J. Sibree, Prometheus Books, 1991.

Jones, M. B., Donnelly, A. and Fabrizio, A. (2006), Responses of Irish vegetation to future climate change, *Biology and Environment*, Proc. R. Ir. Acad. 106B (3).

Murphy, E. (1846), *A Treatise on the Agricultural Grasses*, Dublin and London.

Purvis, G., Downey, L., Beever, D., Monahan, F., Sheridan, H., McMahon, B. et al (in prep.), *Development of a sustainably-competitive agriculture*.

Sparks, S. and Self, S. (2005), *Natural hazards: scientific certainties and uncertainties*, Natural Environmental Research Council (briefing note).

CHAPTER FOURTEEN

Housing
Sustainability and Adaptability in the Irish Housing System

Mary Lee Rhodes

Introduction

One might question whether or not a coherent or compelling vision of housing exists today in Irish government or society at large, but there is certainly an identifiable policy and practice trajectory that has persisted over time. This, of course, is the orientation of Irish housing policy and the Irish citizen towards home owner-ship as the preferable tenure option.[1]

Whether this implies that there is a vision of universal home ownership as the utopian social and economic outcome in Ireland is another question. Much of Irish housing policy ad-dresses situations in which ownership is neither preferable (e.g. the recent omnibus legislation on the private rented sector) nor feasible (e.g. the raft of legislation on homelessness and social housing options). In essence, if one were to characterise the vision of housing in Ireland today it would be a rather *laissez-faire* affair – in other words, let people live in whatever they want, wherever they want, as long as they, or the taxpayer, can pay for it.[2] How well this 'vision' has served Ireland and the Irish people is examined briefly in the next section.

1. For a comprehensive discussion of recent housing policy in Ireland see Norris and Winston (2004)
2. The current Irish government statement on housing reads: 'The over-all objective of housing policy is to enable every household to have available an affordable dwelling of good quality, suited to its needs, in a good environment and as far as possible at the tenure of its choice. The general principle underpinning the housing objective is that those who can afford to provide for their housing needs should do so either through home ownership or private rented accommodation and that targeted supports should be available to others having regard to the nature of their need.'
See: http://www.environ.ie/en/DevelopmentandHousing/Housing/HousingPolicy

Where Ireland is today

In the last reported census data (2006), the percentage of households in owner-occupied housing was 73%. This was down
from 77% in 2002, but still higher than all EU-15 countries except
Spain. Nearly half (46%) of all owner-occupied housing was
owned outright; free of any mortgage or other loan. The remaining households were split almost equally across privately rented
accommodation and social housing (provided by local authorities and non-profit housing associations). In addition to the approximately 1.5 million occupied residences counted in the census,
there were also 215,000 vacant dwellings, 50,000 holiday homes
and 11,000 dwellings occupied by 'visitors' on the night of the
census – or an additional 18% over fully occupied residences.

From a position of lagging well behind the EU average of
dwellings per 1000 inhabitants in the early 1990s, housing construction over the last 15 years has brought Ireland much closer
to par with the EU and the number of vacant dwellings suggests
that there is no lack of supply of housing in Ireland today. The
quality of Irish housing in comparison to EU averages is quite
good, both in terms of the building standards and the type of
housing available. In the last comprehensive reports of housing
type and quality in Ireland,[3] Irish housing was better than EU
averages in nearly all quality measures[4] and the type of housing
available in Ireland was largely (90%) detached or semi-de-
tached dwellings, as compared to most other EU countries in
which apartments made up a significant proportion of the total
housing stock. This last feature of Irish housing reflects the oft
repeated preference of Irish citizens to have 'their own front
door'. Finally, the cost of housing measured as a percentage of
household incomes appears reasonable, averaging at only 12%
of total income.[5] When the broader definition of housing costs[6]
used in EU comparisons is considered, Ireland is just under the

---

3. Watson and Williams (2003); Norris and Winston (2004)
4. Quality measures include elements such as hot running water, flush
toilets and dampness.
5. CSO (2006b)
6. Housing costs reported in EU statistics include rent (imputed rent for
owner-occupied housing) and utility costs (i.e. water, electricity, gas
and other fuel).

EU average of 21%.[7] However, private renters in Ireland on average pay significantly more for housing as a percentage of their incomes than do home owners or social housing tenants.[8]

It would appear, then, that in terms of supply, tenure, quality and affordability, the existing pseudo-vision has done well by Irish citizens. Why, then, would we want to change anything?

Current and future concerns in Irish housing
Acknowledging the successes of Irish housing policy and practice does not mean that there are not significant challenges both currently and anticipated for the future. These may be grouped into two main categories: sustainability and adaptability. The challenges under sustainability are largely recognised already and have to do with economic, social and environmental sustainability.[9] The challenge with respect to adaptability requires some explanation, and will also require a significant degree of leadership and innovation in policy-making to address.

1. Sustainability
Sustainability as a concern in housing has been around for a long time, but its precise meaning continues to be a topic of debate and discussion. Its early policy application was in relation to environmental concerns, such as energy usage, CO_2 emissions, and planning practice. These concerns have only increased in recent years with Ireland failing to meet many of the state, EU and/or global targets agreed. The world is heading towards a climate catastrophe and Ireland, like all countries, will need to find innovative ways of reducing waste, energy consumption and CO_2 emissions from all human activities including housing. Other chapters in this book address environmental and planning issues more comprehensively, so it should be sufficient here to acknowledge that they are of key importance to the future of housing and move on.

With respect to social sustainability, there are multiple chal-

7. Federcasa (2006)
8. NESC (2009)
9. For a general definition of these, see United Nations General Assembly (2005), 2005 World Summit Outcome, Resolution A/60/1, adopted by the General Assembly on 15 September 2005.

lenges facing Ireland arising from current housing policy and practice. The first and perhaps most important of these is the increasing inequality of housing allocation across society. Unfortunately, this is a widespread phenomenon across all capitalist societies pursuing market-based economic policies, even when supplemented with 'targeted supports' to those households with insufficient means. Access to basic social services such as housing, health and education is largely determined by income – as is consumption of other discretionary goods and services – and the distribution of incomes is steadily becoming more unequal over time. In the last survey of household income[10] in Ireland, households in the lowest income decile had a gross income below €200/week, while those in the highest income decile had a gross income in excess of €2,000/week[11] – over ten times that of the lowest decile income group. In addition, in the last assessment of housing need in Ireland,[12] there were over 56,000 households who were assessed as being inadequately housed, which was up from 44,000 in 2005 and double the number in 1996. However, this figure represents only those households that are registered with Local Authorities, and others[13] have estimated that this could underestimate actual need by as much as 50%.

Furthermore, as the population ages, a crisis of adequate housing for older people and people with disabilities looms, with estimates of 13,000 additional nursing home beds required by 2021[14] and 'accessible' housing required for 250,000 additional people with disabilities[15] over the same period. Finally, issues around community sustainability have been raised in the recent government housing policy document, 'Delivering Homes, Sustaining Communities'[16] as well as in the NESC report on

10. CSO (2006b)

11. An income 'decile' represents 10% of a population with incomes in the stated range. Income deciles are used to determine the distribution of income across households in a geographic area and to calculate a standard measure of income inequality (i.e. GINI).

12. DoEHLG (2008)

13. O'Sullivan (2004); Drudy and Punch (2005)

14. Layte (2009)

15. Fennell *et al* (2009)

16. In 'Delivering Homes, Sustaining Communities' there appears to be

well-being in Ireland.[17] Community issues related to housing are generally understood to relate to services available to or required by the residents of a community and/or the level of social deprivation experienced by those residents. Issues of this kind, while of real concern, go beyond the scope of this chapter which has a more narrow focus on dwellings and the allocation thereof, rather than the wider community issues that require attention to social and economic policy-making broadly defined.

Which brings us to the last category of sustainability challenges for housing in Ireland – that of economic sustainability. Simply put, economic sustainability is having enough financial resources now and in the future to maintain or improve on current levels of consumption of a given product or service. The current economic crisis and the significant constraints that this has put on government, as well as on private finances, has made it clear that the expansive government spending policies of the recent past are not sustainable. Nor is it the case that the sort of liberal lending policies of Irish banks will be returning in the near future – if ever. Furthermore, it is well accepted by economists and (hopefully) policy-makers that the level of reliance on the construction sector to drive both employment levels and tax revenues is risky and highly volatile.

To give readers a feel for the extraordinary role of the construction industry in the Irish economy during the boom, in 2005 construction in Ireland accounted for nearly 13% of all jobs and 9% of the gross value added.[18] These figures represented

---

an expansion of the focus of housing policy to include communities as well as individual dwellings. Two statements in the Forward to this document provide insight into the nature of this expansion: (1) 'The key objective outlined in the policy framework is to build sustainable communities, and to meet individual accommodation needs in a manner that facilitates and empowers personal choice and autonomy.' (2) 'The ten-year national social partnership agreement provides an important framework to transform the housing sector in Ireland. Over this time we expect to provide more people with access to home ownership through a variety of forms and expand choice through a modernised private rented sector and the availability of good quality social housing options.'

17. NESC (2009)
18. Source: Eurostat 2005

rates that were approximately 50% higher than EU averages at the time. Around the same time, the government was spending €2 billion on housing related programmes, including €1.4 billion on social housing and €0.6 billion on private housing subsidies.[19] While Ireland does not spend as much on housing supports as many other EU countries, it is the case that a large proportion of the housing stock was either built by the local authorities or subsidised partially or completely through various government programmes. However, direct government financing of new social housing dwellings has all but dried up and is being replaced by leasing strategies targeting vacant private sector dwellings. While this may provide additional social housing in the short term, it will not result in additional housing that may subsequently be sold to tenants. In other words, the housing asset base owned by government is likely to decrease over time. Given the high numbers of households on the waiting list for social housing, this does not appear to fulfil the definition of a 'sustainable' (social) housing strategy.

With regard to private sector housing, it is also the case that the financial resources required to maintain current consumption of these goods and services will increasingly come under pressure. Irish banks are in poor shape, undercapitalised and in disrepute and the Irish mortgage market is not large enough to attract global banks in any significant way. So mortgage finance is likely to be hard to come by for the foreseeable future and more expensive generally than in other, larger markets. Service costs such as water, waste, energy, and transport range from nil to expensive and are likely to rise rather than fall over time. The wide range of private sector housing tax supports are also likely to be decreased – if not eliminated – as the Irish Exchequer struggles to plug the huge deficit in the public finances – over 14% of GDP in 2009 – the worst in the EU that year.[20]

All of the challenges described thus far are well documented and relatively easy to comprehend. Of course they will not be easy to solve – if the social, economic and political resistance

19. NESC (2004)
20. To put this deficit in perspective, the average deficit across EU countries in 2009 was expected to be 3.3% of GDP and the deficit limit agreed by all EU countries was 3%.

that has thus far thwarted efforts in the environmental sustain-ability arena is anything to go by. The issue of adaptability in housing referred to earlier, however, is neither well documented nor easy to explain and, depending upon the strategies used to address this issue, may be even more difficult to sell to the Irish government or to the Irish people.

2. Adaptability and resilience

'Adaptability' may be defined as the 'ability of an entity or or-ganism to alter itself or its responses to the changed circum-stances or environment'.[21] Furthermore, adaptability in man-agement theory is a characteristic that increases the chances of survival of the firm in question, by increasing its 'fitness' – or its ability to compete with other firms on a performance landscape consisting of limited resources and a variety of evolutionary op-tions.[22] There is a similar line of research and theory develop-ment in public administration and socio-ecological systems looking at 'resilience' – which has expanded beyond its relatively narrow boundaries in ecology and disaster recovery to be ap-plied to all manner of public institutions and governance struct-ures.[23] Resilience has many definitions, but one that is reason-able for our purposes here is 'how far a system can be perturbed without shifting to a different regime'.[24] The point of this line of research is to discover the characteristics of systems that make them able to withstand significant shocks or changes – be these environmental, social, financial or whatever. In both areas of in-quiry, the degree of diversity of and interconnectedness among entities, the ability to experiment with new strategies, the free-dom to abandon unsuccessful strategies, the existence of nega-tive feedback loops (or 'checks and balances' in public adminis-tration language) and the achievement of 'requisite variety'[25] be-

21. Source: http://www.businessdicationary.com/definition/adapt-ability.html
22. See Carley (1997), pp 25-47, Levinthal (1997), pp 934-950, Siggelkow and Levinthal (2003), pp 650-669, Siggelkow and Rivkin (2005), pp 101-122
23. See Walker *et al* (2006), pp 12-16, and Toonen (2010), pp 193-202
24. Holling (1973), pp 1-23
25. Ashby (1956). The 'law of requisite variety' was proposed by W. Ross Ashby in 1956 in relation to information theory and the need to

tween a system and its environment have all been proposed as key features of human systems that are adaptable/resilient. In effect, to survive in a changing environment, or in an environment in which there are other entities competing for resources, any system has a better chance if it has these features. The question is what would a housing system with these features look like?

To summarise, we have three main challenges to address in a new vision of Irish housing: (1) to maintain and possibly improve upon the achievements in the areas of quality, supply, affordability and ownership; (2) to achieve sustainability environmentally, socially and economically; and (3) to create a housing system that is adaptable and can meet the first two challenges over time.

A new housing vision for Ireland

A boring vision would simply repeat the above list of challenges and propose that we meet them. But boring visions don't inspire anyone and don't attract the kind of political and social support required to make significant change. Instead, we need a vision that inspires, is easy to remember and is possible to act upon. In that vein, I propose something along the following lines:

> Housing in Ireland must contribute in a fair manner to the well-being of all residents of the State, now and into the future.

An aspirational vision to be sure, but not inconsistent with a groundswell of opinion from economists, social scientists, public policy analysts and others concerning how societies and governments need to reorient themselves towards new measures of social progress. In September 2009, Joseph Stiglitz – a Nobel Prize winning economist – and his co-commissionaires provided a comprehensive set of recommendations on just such a reorientation at the request of President Sarkozy of France. In essence, and in the words of the report writers themselves, 'the report

---

deal with 'noise' in a communications system. This law has evolved over time to have a more general application to systems and may be stated as: 'the larger the variety of actions available to a control system, the larger the variety of perturbations it is able to compensate. (Principia Cybernetica Web, See http://pcp.lanl.gov/reqvar.html)

advocates a shift of emphasis from a 'production-oriented' measurement system to one focused on the well-being of current
and future generations, that is, toward broader measures of
social progress'.[26] While the focus of the report is on measurement, its context is the desire by the French government to establish better bases for the formulation of policies given the
financial, social and political crises facing Europe and the world.
Around the same time in Ireland, a report from the National
Economic and Social Council[27] advocated a similar shift in how
policy and social progress should be measured. Addressing
many of the same dimensions of well-being as the Stiglitz report, it also included recommendations on institutional changes
that needed to occur in order to deliver the sorts of policies and
implementation changes required. This chapter includes a few
of these recommendations, but as it has a more specific focus (on
housing) than the NESC report, the recommendations are corre-
spondingly more specific than those found in either the NESC
report or the Stiglitz report.

Firstly, we need a (set of) measure(s) that indicate how well
housing contributes to well-being. From decades of studies we
know that home ownership, quality and affordability are all factors that contribute to people's satisfaction with their accommodation. Location also appears to be correlated with satisfaction[28]
and this dimension is likely to be related to several indicators of
'community' well-being proposed in the NESC 2009 report – for
example, services available, links to neighbours, and commuting distance. Whatever measures are chosen, they will not be the
ones currently used in policy documents and the press (e.g.
housing completions, local authority waiting lists and house
prices). Taking a relatively simple public value approach government could adopt a 'do no harm' approach and aim to either
improve on the selected outcome indicators without increasing
cost, or deliver the same outcomes for less (public) money.
However, this will not, by itself, address the issues faced by
those who live in inadequate housing today.

---

26. Stiglitz *et al* (2009), p 10
27. NESC (2009)
28. Watson and Williams (2003)

This brings us to the 'fair manner' element of the vision. As was highlighted earlier, the allocation of housing is becoming more unequal, even though the average cost (measured as a percentage of income) appears to be fairly consistent across income ranges.[29] Housing policy needs to address this as a matter of urgency lest the more vulnerable members of society – including older people, people with disabilities, people living in poverty, and children and adults leaving institutions – are left in unsuitable or even degrading accommodation. This will cost money, of course, and given the state of the public finances it would be irresponsible to propose policy interventions without explaining where the money should come from.

Addressing where the money should come from to provide adequate housing for all residents is linked to the overall question of economic sustainability. We need a tax and spend system in housing that is designed to support itself, and this will require that the public revenues generated via housing are, over time, equal to the cost of supporting a 'fair' housing system. This is not difficult to conceive of – it is called 'property tax'. The vast majority of states in the world assess property owners with a tax on the value of their property to support a whole range of public services – including, but not limited to housing. The elimination of property tax in Ireland was a political and economic travesty and it will certainly be reintroduced in the future. In the context of the crisis in finances and a government that has little to lose by being innovative, we have a golden opportunity to improve on the housing system's adaptability and resilience by simplifying the tax and incentive structures in housing finance and shifting the balance of taxation in housing to property (and capital gains) tax and away from transaction tax (i.e. stamp duty) and mortgage relief. The arguments for this are better left to economists (and they have waxed eloquent on this point),[30] so I will simply lay out the basic principle for levying the tax in order to support the vision above.

Property tax levels should be set at a percentage of property

29. CSO (2006b)
30. For those interesting in reading a good summary of the arguments see Commission on Taxation Report 2009, Section 6. Available from http://www.commissionontaxation.ie

value which, in the aggregate, can pay for: (1) basic municipal
services (if these cannot be charged on a usage basis), (2) ongoing reductions in the environmental impact of residential living,
and (3) ongoing provision of suitable housing to people who
cannot afford it through their own means. This should be supplemented with a planning gain or 'windfall profits' tax as proposed in the recent 'Commission on Taxation Report 2009' (see
earlier footnote). The Commission on Taxation's analysis suggested that a 0.25% rate of tax would generate roughly €1 billion
in revenues, so it remains to be seen whether this is sufficient to
pay for the three housing related expenditure categories listed
above. A useful systemic feature of this sort of tax regime is that,
as property increases in value – and becomes more difficult for
people on low incomes to afford – the property tax revenues increase allowing for greater subsidies to be provided.

The above tax recommendation also addresses the challenge
of environmental sustainability in so far as policy-makers establish objectives in relation to the reduction of the environmental
'footprint' of residential living, as well as residential construction. Property tax could be used to pay for the former and, possibly, a proportion of the latter, but there might also be a tax/fine
levied on builders who do not achieve energy or waste targets
set in relation to construction. Overall, however – and similarly
to the case of municipal services – the preferable system as regards environmental impact is one in which the 'polluter pays'
in so far as it is possible.

The other main recommendation with respect to the environment is to ensure that the planning system operates as it is meant
to and is not subject to the sort of corrupt or incompetent practices
that have sadly been a feature of this system from its inception.

This brings us to the final two recommendations which address the challenge of facilitating adaptability of the housing
system overall. The first of these is to increase the diversity of
agents in the housing system by establishing a legal and institutional basis for the existence of 'social enterprises' along the
lines of the recommendations in the 'Report of the Social
Enterprise Task Force'.[31] While there are already various differ-

31. Clann Credo (2010)

ent legal structures for housing provision (e.g. owner-occupiers, local authorities, private landlords, for-profit firms, trusts, housing associations and housing co-operatives), there is no legal structure that would allow an entity to access both public and private funds, and work across both the market and non-market segments of the housing system. Social housing organisations (and charities) operate in the non-market space, while firms and private owners operate in the market space. Those operating in the market cannot access public funds to provide social housing and social housing organisations are prohibited from selling their housing assets on the market to generate funds. In addition to restricting the flexibility and potential for innovation of housing providers, this dual system also has the effect of marginalising the social housing sector.[32] Other jurisdictions, notably the Netherlands and Germany, have models for this type of activity so Ireland would not have to start from a blank sheet of paper in designing how they would work.

The last recommendation is by far the most radical of all, in that it flies in the face of fundamental political and even basic human instincts. Once we create an organisation or a law or any other institution we are loathe to destroy it – particularly if there are people whose livelihoods and/or egos are tied up in its on-going existence. Nevertheless, the byzantine infrastructure of housing related taxes, incentives, schemes, programmes, agencies, regulations and the rest is far too complex, contradictory and costly for a small state such as Ireland to manage effectively. We should apply the principle of Ockham's Razor[33] to the evaluation of whether we need all of the institutions that we have created over the last 100 years or so and eliminate whatever no longer is required.

The recommendations in this section provide a place to start in determining what might be needed going forward. Anything else should be seriously examined to see if it is necessary to achieve the vision. If not, it should be eliminated. Complex

32. Kemeny (1995)
33. Ockham's Razor refers to the principle, attributed to the 14th century logician, William of Ockham, that *Entia non sunt multiplicanda praeter necessitatem* or 'Entities should not be multiplied unnecessarily.' Source: http://en.wikipedia.org/wiki/Occam's_razor

systems do not need complex rules to survive and thrive. Furthermore, the simpler the rules, the easier it is for participants in a system to understand their opportunities and constraints and to explore the 'possibility space' of action. Ireland is filled with creative, motivated people – give them the opportunity to create a new housing system that is fair today and into the future.

References:

Ashby, W. R. (1956), *Introduction to Cybernetics*, NY: Wiley.

Carley, K. (1997), 'Organisational Adaptation', *Annals of Operations Research*, 75 (0).

Central Statistics Office (CSO) (2006a), *Census Preliminary Report*, Dublin: CSO.

Central Statistics Office (CSO) (2006b), *Household Budget Survey 2004-2005*, Dublin: CSO.

Clann Credo (2010), *Adding Value, Delivering Change: The role of social enterprise in national recovery*. Dublin: Clann Credo. Available from http://www.clanncredo.ie/gfx/uploads/textbox/SETFBrochureSml_07_06.pdf.

Department of Environment, Housing and Local Government (2008), *Housing Needs Assessment 2008*, Dublin: DoEHLG.

Drudy, P. J. and Punch, M. (2005), *Out of reach: inequalities in the Irish housing system*, Dublin: TASC at New Island.

Federcasa (2006), *Housing Statistics in the EU 2005/2006*, Rome: CSR.

Fennell, A., Owens, H., Owens, T., Rhodes, ML and Dyer, M. (2009), *Report on the Potential Role of the Private Rented Sector in the Provision of Accommodation for People with Disabilities*, Centre for Housing Research.

Holling, C. S. (1973), Resilience and stability of ecological systems, *Annual Review of Ecology and Systematics* 4.

Kemeny, J. (1995), *From Public Housing to the Social Market. Rental Policy Strategies in Comparative Perspective*, London: Routledge.

Layte, R. (ed), (2009), *Projecting the Impact of Demographic Change on the Demand for and Delivery of Health Care in Ireland*, Ireland: ESRI Research Series 13.

Levinthal, D. (1997), Adaptation on Rugged Landscapes, *Management Science*, 43 (7).

National Economic and Social Council (NESC) (2004), *Housing in Ireland: Performance and Policy*, Dublin: National Economic & Social Council Office.

National Economic and Social Council (NESC) (2009), *Well-being Matters: A Social Report for Ireland*, Dublin: National Economic & Social Council Office.

Norris, M. and Winston, N. (2004), *Housing Policy Review 1990-2003*, Dublin: Stationery Office.

O'Sullivan, E. (2004), *National Report for the Republic of Ireland, 2003-2004: Data, Policy and Research Update*, European Observatory on Homelessness: Feantsa.

Siggelkow, N. and Levinthal, D. (2003), Temporarily Divide to Conquer: Centralized, Decentralized, and Reintegrated Organizational Approaches to Exploration and Adaptation, *Organization Science*, 14 (6).

Siggelkow, N. and Rivkin, J. (2005), Speed and Search: Designing Organizations for Turbulence and Complexity, *Organization Science*, 16 (2).

Stiglitz, J., Sen, A. and Fitoussi, J-P. (2009), *Report by the Commission on the Measurement of Economic Performance and Social Progress*. Available from http://www.stiglitz-sen-fitoussi.fr/documents/rapport_anglais.pdf

Toonen, T. (2010), Resilience in Public Administration: The Work of Elinor and Vincent Ostrom from a Public Administration Perspective, *Public Administration Review*, 70 (2).

Walker, B. H., Anderies, J. M., Kinzig, A. P. and Ryan, P. (2006), Exploring Resilience in Social-Ecological Systems Through Comparative Studies and Theory Development: Introduction to the Special Issue, *Ecology and Society*, 11 (1).

Watson, D. and Williams, J. (2003), *Irish National Survey of Housing Quality 2001-2002*, Dublin: Economic and Social Research Institute.

CHAPTER FIFTEEN

Landscape and Heritage
An Act of Kindness for All Our Landscapes

Michael Starrett

Introduction

In 10 years I have seen the Heritage Council landscape agenda emerge from the wilderness to become a mainstream European and national policy objective through the Irish ratification of the European Landscape Convention[1] and the Irish government's commitment in the 2007 Programme for Government, reaffirmed in 2009, to develop a National Landscape Strategy.

Also in the intervening period the Irish landscape has been the stage on which our economic boom was played and went bust. In 1999 speaking at the Heritage Council's first major landscape conference in Tullamore[2] Fred Aalen warned:

> Serious damage to our landscape and the environment must be anticipated when dynamic economic growth occurs in a country with a weak planning system and poorly developed environmental policies.

Ten years after Aalen's prophetic words, the Heritage Council held its second international landscape conference,[3] not primarily to look back over the events of the intervening years, rather to seek to influence the agenda for the next ten. This chapter, in referring to the second conference, draws too on the work contained in documentation in preparation by the Heritage Council as a response to the government's consultative draft of the National Landscape Strategy.

All of this work seeks to strengthen the links and connections between heritage and landscape. Our heritage, our landscape.

---

1. Council of Europe, European Landscape Convention. See: www. coe.int/t/dg4/cultural heritage/conventions.
2. Heritage Council Series (1999)
3. Heritage Council (2009)

A human construct

Heritage is a human construct or, said in everyday terms, it is devised by, influenced by, and concerns people. The Heritage Act (1995) under which the Heritage Council was established, defines heritage in a broad sense, including all aspects of our natural and cultural heritage. Most importantly that definition includes our landscapes. The connection between people and the landscapes in which they live work and play should be self evident and yet as stated by Freda Rountree,[4] the Heritage Council's first Chairperson, people have been disenfranchised from their heritage, and by implication their landscape. It has been something of a mission to correct that wrong.

Where we all live, work and relax

The Irish landscape[5] is after all where we all live, work and spend our recreation time. In towns and cities and villages, in suburbia, in the countryside, along the coast or when at sea the landscape is what surrounds us all day, every day. It is the entirety of our surroundings. We own it, rent it or enjoy just passing through it. It is ours to use for better or worse. It has both economic and spiritual value. It is at the same time mythical and real and is a vital resource. It is the foundation of good living space and contributes to our health and sense of well-being. It is shared and exploited by man, by plants and by animals. Landscape occupies a central place in our culture and in our nature, and it can be argued that it defines our natural and cultural identity. This identity can be articulated in our own character and found in specific place names and townland names that persist through each new generation. In short, the landscape provides us with a vital resource that we use to sustain ourselves physically and spiritually.

Few would disagree with the fact that placed in the above context, our landscapes today face an increasingly complex range of challenges. These challenges were the subject of the

4. Freda Rountree 1954-2000. *Pers. comm.*
5. The meaning of the term landscape as defined in the European Landscape Convention is 'an area as perceived by people, whose character is the result of the action and interaction of natural and/or human factors (ELC Article 1)

Heritage Council's Landscape Conference held in October 2009, a conference that brought together a broad range of communities with an interest in the future planning, management and conservation of their landscapes. Building on the framework provided by the European Landscape Convention, the conference saw the opportunity for a new way of working and thinking about our landscape, one whereby we place people and their active participation in shaping their landscape in a central position.

We may use the landscape to sustain us but we have learned some very painful lessons in the last decade that to use it without understanding, without respect for the non-renewable form of its resources, leads to our own impoverishment socially, environmentally and economically.

Whether through the recent experiences we have had with an unsustainable form of economic growth, the accelerating natural and manmade impacts of climate change or the demands of an increasingly urbanised society on our natural and cultural resources, there are major issues that need to be resolved and changes made in how we legislate for, plan, manage and conserve our landscapes today and in the future.

Any doubts that there is need for change can be dispelled by a quick visit to one of the country's new ghost estates, or an examination of the new postal addresses[6] in Ireland since 2005 that have contributed to the unmeasured change in character of many rural and urban landscapes. The connection between unsustainable economic developments and the health and wellbeing of our society and the landscapes in which we live are all too starkly illustrated by examples such as the spectre of unemployment and the general decline in our water quality (including drinking water). Add to that the invasion of abandoned farm land by scrub, the general deterioration in our biodiversity,[7] and loss of many archaeological features,[8] or make a visit to the extensive areas that are still recoiling from the flooding in late 2009 in urban and rural environments and you will soon appreciate aspects of the economic, social and environmental difficulties that we have created for ourselves.

6. Heritage Council (2009), Fig 6, p 117
7. National Parks and Wildlife Service (2008)
8. Heritage Council (2001)

Following Convention

In all this gloom there is real room for optimism. There is a need to confront reality and find proposals that taken collectively can help to resolve the issues surrounding our rural, urban and peri-urban landscapes. Any new proposals must reflect new ideas regarding how we can work more closely with people to manage, plan and conserve all of Ireland's landscapes and provide them with information, structures and frameworks to do so. We have help in the form of the European Landscape Convention. The Heritage Council and many of its European partners have been working over a ten-year period to promote the 'all landscapes' approach advocated in the European Landscape Convention and to demonstrate through a number of its own initiatives just what is possible.

The Convention includes urban, rural and peri-urban landscapes and, with all its very positive specific and general measures, provides a framework for those States that have ratified it to empower and enable people and communities to be active in the planning, management and conservation of their landscapes. The Convention is non-prescriptive. Depending on the needs of particular countries the convention requires actions within new or modified frameworks that ultimately assist in delivering true economic, environmental and social benefits for everyone involved, i.e. sustainable development in its purist form.

The following paragraphs offer examples of how the Heritage Council has nurtured local and community initiatives in Ireland to emphasise the importance of community participation in the planning, management and conservation of our landscapes. These build on examples and solutions that other European Countries have applied to assist in their implementation of the ELC and the delivery of those economic, environmental and social benefits through the landscape approach.

It has to be said in looking at frameworks and structures within which to establish such initiatives, and in comparison to other European partners, Ireland has a fairly clean sheet on which to build. It is only with the emergence of the 2010 Planning Bill that we will see our landscape defined in primary planning legislation, or in the development of our new National Monuments Legislation that recognition will be given to

Historic Landscapes. Significantly our primary protected land-scapes, our National Parks, exist within no specific legislative framework other than ownership by the State.

Community Participation in planning, management and conservation of the landscape

The Heritage Council, in supporting the following initiatives, aims to increase the awareness of the value of all the landscapes in which we live everyday and indeed emphasises the right of people to identify with their landscape and exercise their duty of care for it. Something as all-encompassing as our landscape deserves to be treated well. If we treat it well it brings us a good quality of life, health, prosperity and allows us to pass it on in a better condition than that in which we inherited it. This is for us, for our future and that of our children and their children's child-ren.

The following examples, dealt with briefly here, illustrate the highs and lows of introducing new concepts. They show the willingness and commitment of local communities to become involved and highlight their frustrations in dealing with exist-ing frameworks and structures that they perceive pay only lip service to their participation in the process. Above all they show what could be achieved if similar supports and structures were more widely available.

Each of the examples is covered in much more detail in the published papers from the Heritage Council's 2009 Landscape Conference.[9] It is also important to say that none of these studies is complete or presented as a success for others to follow. They are models that may have application in particular sets of cir-cumstances, if communities see the need. More importantly, if Ireland is to truly implement the European Landscape Con-vention effectively the structures and frameworks within which these communities have derived benefits need to be strength-ened and given a wider application. The examples are mainly representative of steps taken within our rural landscapes but other community initiatives that Council has supported in our towns, our villages and our cities in association with many part-

9. Heritage Council (2009), pp 193-218

ners can be accessed on the Heritage Council website in documentation referred to as Landscape Factsheets.

The Wicklow Uplands Council
The Wicklow Uplands Council (WUC) has existed and brought benefits to its stakeholders for over 10 years. The Heritage Council has supported it during all that period exactly because local communities and sectoral interests came together to work for a common goal. That goal can be summarised as local people working together to secure an integrated approach to landscape management and conservation in the Wicklow Uplands. And all of this before the publication of the European Landscape Convention in Florence in 2000. Local people galvanised to work together as a result of the threatened imposition of a major interpretative centre at Luggala.

The Wicklow Uplands Council works for all landscapes. Towns and villages, forest or moorland are all part of the rich mosaic. There is no line drawn on a map.

Speaking at Tullamore in 2009, Colin Murphy, the Council's Director stated that the story of the Council

> ... reflects a journey over the past 10 years. The story attempts to explain what has happened with this unique experiment in 'landscape management by consensus' and, looking ahead, a view of the horizon ...

Speaking on behalf of the membership, Murphy gave a refreshingly honest and forthright view of the highs and lows. Such highs and lows are not surprising when you consider the membership comprises more than 20 local and national organisations and a similar number of individual members. They are organised in four panels, namely:
- Farming and Landowning
- Environmental and Recreational
- Community
- Economic and Tourism

These are the themes that local people agreed were significant in allowing WUC to work towards consensus on an agreed objective, namely:

To work towards the sustainable use and enjoyment of the landscape in partnership with those who live, work and recreate there.

Their achievements since the publication of their first three year plan 2000-2002 have been considerable. These have included:
- negotiated access over private land,
- supporting on-farm accommodation,
- environmental and heritage educational initiatives,
- the PURE project – Protecting the Uplands Rural Environment from litter and illegal dumping and
- projects with the Wicklow Private Woodlands Owners' Group.

The Heritage Council has provided core funding and additional project support. WUC has as a result secured additional funding over the years that has multiplied the available financial resource from the Heritage Council approximately fourfold. In short, a request from local people for small scale funding and granted by the Heritage Council has allowed them to secure much greater resources and more importantly allowed them to do what they have agreed to do in their landscape.

Of course all of this is achieved in a legislative and structural vacuum and is restricted to a small number of areas in Ireland as a result. It has worked because local people wanted it and the Heritage Council had a limited amount of core funding to allocate to it. As a pilot it has been a success but how can we secure similar benefits for a much broader range of communities and their heritage, including their landscapes? In a vacuum, the ability to maintain such success is very fragile.

As long ago as 2005 my views on the need for new legislative frameworks were published and known.[10] In sharing these views as a means to expand the benefits available to the Wicklow Uplands Council, my calls for new legislation were misrepresented as seeking to impose an expansion of the Wicklow National Park to private land. Nothing could have been further from the truth. It may have suited some to present my views as such and in the intervening 5 years I have worked

---

10. Starrett (2005)

very hard, together with all groups involved in the WUC to explain the potential of new legislation that empowers and enables rather than imposes. As I write, confidence exists (and has been re-established) between the membership of WUC and myself that such a proposal could assist in providing longer term support mechanisms for WUC and indeed a much wider group of similar bodies across the Irish Landscape. However experience to date surrounding the imposition of regulatory legislation clouds people's capacity to believe that legislation could work in another way. As WUC is currently carrying out its own review to inform its direction over the next ten years, it will remain well placed to benefit should new approaches emerge in the wake of the Government's National Landscape Strategy.

A Charter for the Burren – imagine that!
The Burren has over generations provided support and sustenance for many families. It has provided the hard won soil and water of quality to support them and provide a quality of life that many would envy. It has at the same time provided inspiration for writers and poets and visitors who marvelled at the dynamic and changing nature of this landscape, who all, just like its residents, drew strength and inspiration from its ever-changing vistas and the feeling that this was at the same time the harshest and most gentle of places. The variety of plants and animals that it could support has long been recognised as of international significance and the Burren is undoubtedly one of our most iconic landscapes. The international recognition accorded to the Burren, and the richness of its cultural / people's landscape extends interest in its future well-being well beyond the narrow confines of our shores.

Now, close your eyes and imagine that an agreement was in place that provided the opportunity for everyone who valued the Burren to work together and put together an agreed action plan. That action plan when implemented would bring benefits of an economic, social and environmental nature to all those who live in, work in and visit the Burren. That programme would, if you close your eyes even further, have dedicated support structures and human and financial resources to make it happen and regular reviews and evaluations to make sure it was doing just that in the way that people wanted. Imagine even more. This action plan, this programme, the benefits derived from it, the structures and resources to be given to it were not imposed on those who live, work or play in the Burren, but were provided because the people wanted them and a framework existed at a national level to bring people together (if they wanted) and then to support them when they did. This level of empowerment and enabling of such regional and local communities to manage and conserve their landscapes requires a whole new way of working and indeed thinking and yet its conception is so simple.

It represents, in fact embodies the participative approach promoted by the European Landscape Convention.

I hear you humming the words of John Lennon's song *Imagine* and the line 'They may say that I'm a dreamer ...' My riposte is equally quick with 'well, I'm not the only one ...' My earnest commitment now that we have opened our eyes is that with a bit of imagination, and some leadership, the new way of working is only just around the corner.

Heaven knows that there have been enough economic, environmental and social upheavals in Ireland in general in recent times to suggest we have to do something differently. The Burren can take the lead.

It is in this context that the idea of a Burren Charter has been conceived. New momentum has been added to the need for such a mechanism following the impassioned plea of Michael Davoren at the landscape Conference in October 2009 on behalf of the Burren IFA. Many groups and individuals are carrying out excellent work in the Burren, all of which has an impact on the management and conservation of their landscape and of course on the people who live in, work in and visit that landscape. Whilst all of these groups do their level best to communicate effectively, much of the good and benefit to be derived from their work is threatened by the fact that they are only working on short term projects. Their funding from Europe or other sources is only short term and the main energy has to be directed not to doing the work that is required for the benefit of everyone in the long term, but in wondering from where the next source of funding might come. Surely Ireland really has gone beyond such a hand to mouth type of existence.

The framework for a Burren Charter is in its very early stages of development. The Heritage Council has over the last few years been involved in supporting a wide range of initiatives through its grants programmes and at the same time has met with and discussed the possibility of such a Charter with representatives of a range of groups including the local authority, the Burren IFA, Burrenbeo, Burren Connect, Shannon Development and government departments. Notwithstanding the current economic situation, the Heritage Council has secured resources to allow the Charter to develop further in 2010.

A variety of surveys and reports have been carried out locally and my overwhelming sense is that people are supportive of the idea and we now need to capture the imagination. However, if the Heritage Council is to be true to its principles regarding the desire to enable and empower regional and local communities, to truly devolve responsibility and allow those communities to identify and agree what they want for their landscapes, this Charter cannot be imposed. It has to be requested. The value and need for it has to be recognised. All the Heritage Council should do is say the mechanism exists and please use it if you can all agree on what you want.

Such a change in how we go about doing our business together cannot be rushed. It requires real and meaningful levels of participation in the process. There is of course ultimately the need for leadership at a national level if such mechanisms and structures are to be sustainable in the future. The government's commitment to put a National Landscape Strategy in place during 2010, reiterated at the Heritage Council's landscape conference in Tullamore in October 2009, can provide that leadership.

Let's hope that our imagination allows us to grasp the opportunity and when we look back in ten years' time that we can all see clearly the benefit from such a change.

The Tara/Skryne Landscape Conservation Area

In August 2007, Mr John Gormley TD, Minister for the Environment, Heritage and Local Government, accepted a Heritage Council proposal to use Section 204 of the 2000 Planning Act to designate a Landscape Conservation Area in the Tara/Skryne Valley. The proposal came in the wake of the decision to build the M3

motorway in the valley and was presented by the Heritage
Council as a positive step, a means, to recognise the ongoing significance and value of the area. Having made its view known
that the route was not one Council itself would have chosen,
Council still recognised the value of the landscape and its ongoing significance, the presence of the new motorway notwithstanding. It was still a special landscape.

The policy framework to develop such a proposal is contained in the County Meath Development Plan 2007-2013 and
the main partners in the designation process are Meath County
Council, the Department of Environment, Heritage and Local
Government and the Heritage Council. It was agreed by all partners that the proposal would test the provisions within the
Planning Act 2000 that enable planning authorities to designate
a Landscape Conservation Area and to evaluate it as a mechanism for the delivery of a proactive approach to landscape management.

In effect the proposal was testing whether planning legislation and its application to secure the strongest available level of
landscape protection available in Ireland, could also be harnessed through effective public participation to deliver agreed
actions on landscape management.

Speaking at the 2009 Tullamore conference, the project co-or-
dinator Dr Loreto Guinan highlighted the details of her work,
breaking down the programme into three distinct phases, namely:
-    Phase One (Conception and Research)
-    Phase Two (Public Participation)
-    Phase Three (Management Plan)

Guinan went on to say that the Tara Skryne Landscape will
continue to evolve over time and the challenge is to influence
and manage this change in a positive and sustainable manner
that can deliver economic, social and environmental benefits
such as employment, health, education, recreation and a high
quality environment. She concluded that we must also ensure
that future generations have the opportunity to learn from, appreciate and enjoy the character and values of this special place.

This returns us clearly to our starting point – that we use
landscape to sustain us. If we want to continue to do so for future
generations we must use it sustainably and people who live in,

work in and visit that landscape must be involved in the process. In May 2010 the order designating the Landscape Conservation Area was published while the work on public participation and the management plan development are ongoing.

The outcome of the public consultation and the decision of Meath County Council are eagerly awaited.

Conclusion

I think we can all recognise the serious damage to landscape and environment that has been fuelled in the last decade by the turbo-charged development of this country. There is still time to act – to make a difference. We need to find a new way of working. There is still sufficient quality remaining in our rural, urban and peri-urban landscape for us to be optimistic that we can treat those landscapes, the heritage they contain and ourselves more appropriately in the future. We are after all doing this for ourselves. We live in, work in and play in this Irish landscape and its quality affects all our lives individually and collectively.

There are too many examples which could be used to show how easily good intent can be derailed by lack of meaningful public participation. These serve to illustrate just how essential it is to secure in Ireland a new approach to landscape management and conservation where public participation is meaningful. Despite the warnings from the Heritage Council and others about the overwhelming importance of landscapes to the communities that live within them, and the need to fully involve them in the decision-making process, we still continue to disenfranchise people and allow them to perceive that their input is neither significant nor important.

However, the above examples from Wicklow, Clare and Meath have highlighted that with a little imagination and a little resource new ways of working are possible.

It is unfortunate in a developed democracy such as Ireland that we still seem to lack that imagination and that resource for the country as a whole. Yet I remain optimistic that an opportunity is currently presented through our ratification of the European Landscape Convention and our government's commitment to develop a National Landscape Strategy.

Despite the fact that democracies work through legislating

for what is important to them, it is unlikely that the strategy will initially embrace new landscape legislation to empower and enable local communities to take landscape management and conservation initiatives on a landscape scale. Testing existing legislation to see whether it can deliver such objectives is a softer and much more conservative option.

Nonetheless my commitment to the need for a Landscape Ireland Act remains undiminished. The direction advocated in this new style of legislation turns our traditional approach of designation from 'on high' on its head. As one member of a local community described it – you mean '*à la carte* legislation' – where each and every different landscape could through the people who live there, work there or indeed just visit – benefit from a structure dedicated to delivering an agreed range of activities and actions. A Landscape Ireland Act would allow the social, environmental and economic benefits from such an approach to be more evenly and widely distributed and available. It might even allow charters such as that proposed for the Burren, or stakeholder groups such as that in Wicklow, or the management plan in development for the Tara/Skryne Valley enjoy benefits on a long term basis.

As models to show others what is possible when we connect people to their landscape and their heritage that is the very least they deserve.

References:

Heritage Council (2001), *Archaeological Features at Risk*, Kilkenny: Heritage Council.

Heritage Council (2009), *The Irish Landscape 2009; Looking Around, Looking Ahead* (Conference Papers), Heritage Council.

Heritage Council Series (1999), *Towards Policies and Proposals for the Irish Landscape*, Kilkenny: Heritage Council.

National Parks and Wildlife Service (2008), *Conservation Status in Ireland of Habitats and Species Listed in the European Council Directive on the Conservation of Habitats, Flora and Fauna*, Dept of the Environment, Heritage and Local Government.

Starrett, M. (2005), Landscape, Legislation and a Healthy Heritage, *Heritage Outlook* 9.

CHAPTER SIXTEEN

Spatial Planning
A Vision of Contrasts

Hendrik W van der Kamp

A Vision of Contrasts

The vision for a future Ireland that is presented here is a vision of an Ireland that retains its contrasts. A vision that avoids a pattern of development that will ultimately lead to a degree of 'sameness' throughout the country. An Ireland where, as a result of urban development, the contrasts gradually disappear that traditionally exist between city and countryside, between village and the rural hinterland, and between the urban areas and the pristine landscapes. Instead, it should be an objective to keep the contrasts between the different types of landscapes and between the urban and the rural areas. Ideally, it should be an objective also to keep cities and towns themselves distinctive through expressing local character and identity.

Such a sense of physical and environmental characteristics that define the local landscape of both town and countryside is at risk. The experience of the last few decades has seen development moving towards a 'sameness' throughout the country which is to the detriment ultimately not only of the Irish countryside and its cities but also of international competitiveness and quality of life. This trend towards a common appearance of both the urban and rural environment is evident in our shopping centres where local family-based businesses are increasingly being replaced by international retail chains (with the effect that the shopping streets of our cities loose local distinctiveness), in the abundance of one-off housing throughout all rural parts of the country, in the loss of crisp edges between the urban area and the rural hinterland and in the construction of a type of single family housing throughout the country that displays a sense of uniformity and lack of design quality.

Polycentric Lifestyles need Polycentric Cities

To achieve an Ireland where contrasts prevail will require planning and a clear and explicit vision of the type of Ireland that we want. One way in which such a vision can be achieved is by adopting a policy towards 'polycentric urban development'. This means that city regions comprise a range of settlements of different sizes, connected with each other but together forming an urban entity. In order to appreciate the importance of such an urban model it is useful to distinguish between three types of urban development. The first is that of the traditional compact city. This is the city where living and working are mixed so that the inhabitants are able to live at a reasonable distance from their work and satisfy most of their mobility needs within a distance range that can be satisfied by using public transport combined with cycling and walking. Such a city, while often aspired to in official policy documents, in reality has been replaced with a city where there has been a functional separation between working (in the centre) and residential (in the suburbs) leading to urban sprawl and increased travel distances between the home and the place of work, often requiring car based travel. The dominant type of mobility in this type of city is commuting directed predominantly in one direction (into the city in the morning peak and out of the city in the evening peak). This second model of urban sprawl is often criticised and blamed for many of the ills that we are currently experiencing. In its place we would like to see a return to the compact city model, but is that a realistic option?

A third model is the polycentric city, where the city is comprised of a number of urban settlements, connected to each other by good transport systems and together forming a city region. While each of the urban settlements within the network may in themselves be compact and comprising mixed land use, the urban residents often display a lifestyle that can be described as 'polycentric', i.e. they visit different urban settlements for different purposes whether work or leisure based, resulting in a criss-cross travel pattern. This polycentric lifestyle is a reality that should be recognised.

The City State Model

How many of such polycentric cities can we create? Here also it is arguable that Ireland faces a choice between three options: (1) the idea of Balanced Regional Development as envisaged in the National Spatial Strategy (NSS) where another city or cities in the west are stimulated to grow in order to counterbalance Dublin, or (2) a non-planned trend scenario where development takes place all over the country, or (3) concentrating urban development in one large urban network based on the Dublin-Belfast urban network. The first model provides a counter-weight to the Greater Dublin Area in the east. The second model disperses urban development throughout the country thereby failing to create any city of significant size. The third model concentrates the bulk of the national population into one urban area of significant size to compete internationally. In many ways, we can see the results already if the trend scenario were allowed to be continued. Although the NSS tried to concentrate development in a limited number of gateway cities and hub towns, in reality development took place in a more dispersed pattern as a result of continued one-off housing and also significant rezoning policies in smaller settlements throughout the country.

Dublin Belfast Corridor: a polycentric city

It can be argued that Ireland is too small in population size to achieve any more than one international city. Given the proximity of Belfast to Dublin, compared to the next biggest city Cork (167 instead of 257 km), ultimately a single urban corridor along the east coast is both a sensible, efficient and also desirable development option. Instead of trying to compete on size, all other smaller cities and towns should develop niche markets based on strong city regions. The polycentric city model should therefore primarily be focused on an urban corridor along the eastern seaboard, but this does not mean that other cities and towns in other parts of Ireland cannot also be combined into polycentric networks although of much smaller size.

Because of the need to maintain our largest cities of a certain size to be able to compete internationally, and because of the inherent differences in the landscape, infrastructure and soil qualities between the (south)east and (north)west of the island, it is very likely that, over time, Ireland will be broadly divided into a largely urbanised east (and south) of the country and a dispersed settlement pattern of the west (and north) of Ireland.[1] A vision of an urbanised east coast of the country does not mean, however, that the countryside will be lost. A fundamental principle in the polycentric urban network model is the three elements: the individual settlements that together form the network, the connections between them in the form of transport infrastructure, and the open areas in between the settlements. Our main cities and towns should be developed as urban networks integrating the rural hinterland as part of the network rather than treating the rural area as an area of overspill of poorly controlled urban sprawl.

City Region: A New Format for Governance
Policies based on polycentric urban networks require forms of local administration that are appropriate to develop, implement and monitor policies for such areas. This requires cohesive policies for city regions instead of the individual cities. A city region is a spatial unit that is large enough to include the broad social and economic networks of the inhabitants. A typical city region should therefore include most people's commuting distances and should be of sufficient size to compete internationally and / or achieve a clear identity that can be used for international marketing purposes.

This can only be achieved if the governance structures reflect the economic and social units that these city regions represent.

---

1. This was the finding in a study of future scenarios of urban development in Ireland. The study (*Twice the Size? Imagineering the future of Irish Gateways*, Urban Forum, Dublin 2008) used the methodology of 'backcasting'. Based on an assumed picture of Ireland in fifty years' time an analysis was carried out on how likely it was that this situation would be reached. The strength of this technique is that it forces the analyst to identify the changes, events or trends that are likely to happen if the assumed future was to become a reality. In other words: the key is that the analysis is not focused on estimating the likely future situation, but rather on the factors that must occur if an assumed future becomes reality. This methodology led to the clear conclusion that the Dublin-Belfast scenario was out of three scenarios the most robust and likely scenario.

This is currently not the case. A number of the gateway cities designated in the National Spatial Strategy straddle administrative boundaries between city and county authority (e.g. Cork, Limerick or Waterford) or even between different counties (Athlone/Tullamore/Mullingar, Limerick). These difficulties are avoidable if proper local government structures are adopted appropriate for the spatial unit that a modern city region represents. So for example, instead of the current situation of local authorities of Kerry and Cork Counties and Cork City Council, coupled with a South West regional authority which combines the administrative areas of all three, one could imagine a strong Cork City Region. Such an authority should be well placed to compete internationally. In the vision of 'contrasts' such a city region should be clearly identifiable because of the strengths of the region and should be quite different to, say, the Galway or Waterford City Regions.

Strategic Sites
In addition to the three ingredients for a successful polycentric urban network (the settlements, the connections and the open landscapes) there is a fourth. One of the great challenges that the polycentric city model offers to policy makers, is that the city region also comprises so-called 'strategic sites'. Strategic sites are specific locations within the urban region that are for one reason or another particularly suitable for a specific activity. Examples of strategic sites in the Greater Dublin Area could be sites with particularly good transport access (such as a site beside Dublin Airport or where Metro North will intersect with the M50) or sites of particular cultural or landscape value (such as Glendalough or the Boyne Valley). It does not matter why a site is strategic, but once it is recognised to be of strategic significance, such sites require protection and appropriate policies to develop and retain the suitability.

Characteristics that make sites strategic can be lost through inappropriate forms of development. For example, potential industrial sites with deep water access that are perhaps suitable for major chemical industries, can be effectively sterilised by inappropriate low density housing development (bungalows). A site suitable for long distance haulage and logistics type activities may be hampered by inappropriate retail development and the traffic generated by local housing and retail. One of the biggest threats to the protection of strategic sites is perhaps the proliferation of one-off housing throughout the country because where there are houses there are people who can (often legitimately) object to a facility such as a waste incinerator, a large wind farm or overhead electricity pylons, all potentially very important facilities for a modern country.

Green Networks
This vision for Ireland assumes that there is a crisp demarcation between the urban and rural both within the urban networks and between these networks. Settlements should generally be compact in size but well connected with each other to form larger urban networks. By connecting compact towns and cities of varying sizes with each other, one can achieve a number of important objectives in planning. First of all, because each settlement is compact, activities can be close together and the need for long distance car based commuting patterns are avoided. Secondly, by connecting the settlements with good quality public and private transport networks, the objective of 'size' can be achieved. Thirdly, by keeping the individual settlements compact but integrated in urban networks, there is good scope to create green networks of recreation areas that are accessible to the people living in towns and cities.

This means that in a linear urban network such as the Dublin-Belfast corridor, one must not only find specific functions for each of the settlements in the network but also prevent these towns growing together thus reducing the distinctiveness of each of the settlements within the city region. This requires 'positive zoning' of the open areas between the towns. Rather than treating the undeveloped areas outside the settlements as agricultural land without specific zoning, or as a green belt zone which prevents any development taking place, these areas should be treated as part of the city region capable of accommodating many land uses that urban residents require but that are better located in the open areas than in the built up part of the city region. Recognising that urban residents need parks, it is perhaps preferable to provide the park between the settlements thereby strengthening the separation between the urban areas, rather than within the settlement. After all, because the entire network now forms the 'city', such a park is still located within the city to serve its population. Other types of land uses that can be accommodated in the zones between the settlements are: caravan parks, waste facilities, greenhouses, and recreational spaces including horseriding, golf courses and allotments.

Complementarity instead of Competition
We must bring out the contrast between towns rather than hide the differences. This can potentially strengthen an urban net-work compared to policies that are based on individual settle-ments. This can be illustrated with two small towns in West Clare: Lahinch and Ennistymon. Whereas Lahinch has the sea-side, a golf course and holiday homes, Ennistymon can boast a quality traditional townscape, Irish heritage and pubs with music. Together the towns can offer a tourist package that is greater than the sum of the parts. Instead of competing with one another to attract tourists, the towns are better off as an integrated spatial unit with complementary roles. The same principles can also be used for towns of different size within a polycentric urban network. Particularly for smaller towns that are in close proximity to a larger city, it may be difficult to compete in terms of retail or employment. There is a real risk for those smaller towns to become 'sucked' into the urban expansion of the city, or become a 'dormitory town' to the main city where all of the life takes place in the city and the town is confined to offering homes for residents.

However, the smaller town often has characteristics that are special and unique and that can be complementary to the range of activities that the main city can offer. This can be illustrated with the town of Bray. Instead of competing with Dublin City Centre, Bray can develop a niche market based on the seaside and Bray Head. Rather than competing with Dublin's city centre that offers higher order facilities and nightlife, Bray's town cen-tre should develop its retail offer based on the seaside experi-ence. This means that identities need to be identified: e.g. what makes Bray special and distinctive, and what makes it different from Dublin? But equally, how is Bray different from Swords, a similar size town located at a similar distance from Dublin but with very different strategic advantages. While both towns would form part of the eastern corridor polycentric urban network, have similar proximity to Dublin, are of similar size and both have motorway access, there are significant differences. Swords has the airport and forms a county town, whereas Bray has its history, a steady rather than fast-growing population, and the seafront. Differences to be embraced, not hidden.

A Crisp Urban Edge

One of the unintended by-products of the urban expansion process, is the uncertainty that can occur in the so-called 'urban fringe'. More often than not, active agricultural use on land that is located immediately outside the urban development is not feasible as a result of urban activities such as trespass, trampling, or noise. Equally the farmer has not unreasonable expectations that the land might be zoned in the next development plan review. It is arguable that it would be preferable if the edge of the city or town was defined by a clear line beyond which the town would not be expected to expand. The agricultural land adjacent to the urban edge is then less likely to suffer from land speculation or hope value. Also, a range of semi-rural uses could be considered for this zone such as: open space, horse-riding schools, urban farming areas or allotments. Where the town is unlikely to expand further, adjacent agricultural land should be zoned as such instead of treating it like land awaiting rezoning in the next development plan review.

Changes required

How can this vision be achieved? The vision in itself is not something that has a clear implementation target. It may not even have clear policies attached that should be implemented in order to achieve the vision. The vision is more like a 'yardstick', a reference point that can be used whenever a policy decision must be taken. Each time the question must be: if there is a choice between two options, which one of the two is more likely to move towards achieving the vision? That is the one that should generally be favoured. A vision is like a point on the horizon: clearly identifiable and helpful in deciding the course of travel, but it may never be reached.

Looking back over the last few decades, it is easy to see how the policies outlined above would require an approach that is fundamentally different to what we have done in the past. First and foremost, one must adopt integrated spatial planning instead of the sectoral project based approach that we are familiar with. How a project based approach can lead to significant delays can be illustrated by examining some of the large scale infrastructure projects that have been proposed in the Greater Dublin Area in the last two decades and where the development plans in place made little or no reference to these projects. For example:

- The High Court declared in 1998 that a landfill at Ballynagran proposed by Wicklow County Council in its own administrative area, constituted a material contravention of the County Development Plan.
- A planning application by a private developer in 1999 for permission for a toxic waste incinerator at Kilcock, Co Kildare, was refused permission by An Bord Pleanála because the site was deemed 'primarily agricultural' in the County Development Plan.
- An announcement in 1994 of the Minister for Finance approving the so-called Northern Port Access Route (later known as the Dublin Port Tunnel) required a variation of the development plan because the project had not been included in the 1991 City Development Plan.
- In 2005 the Government proposed to relocate an existing prison (Mountjoy prison) in the city of Dublin to a greenfield site north of Dublin (Thornton Hall) on unzoned agricultural land.

Other large scale projects failed and one must question the strategic planning behind these projects. In October 1999 a proposal to extend Dublin Port by reclaiming 21 hectares of land was advertised by the Dublin Port Company but permission was refused in June 2010. In January 2000 a feasibility study of a plan for an 80,000-seat stadium at Abbotstown in north Dublin was presented by the government but it was abandoned in 2004 because of excessive cost. In September 2005, the Dublin Airport Authority outlined plans to build a second terminal to the south of the existing facilities, despite strong lobbying from private developers to build a facility to the west of the airport. Planning permission was granted in August 2007 but only for phase one.

Following a number of failed attempts during the 1990s to locate a National Conference Centre at different locations in Dublin (Phoenix Park racecourse, RDS Ballsbridge, O'Connell Street) the selection of Spencer Dock as the site for the centre was finally confirmed in August 2006.

Instead of policies that adopt an integrated approach for urban and rural areas, planning policies generally have made a distinction between policies for urban areas and for rural areas. For example, we have planning guidelines for urban housing and for rural housing, while local government structures are based on distinction between the city and its rural hinterland rather than treating the hinterland as part of the city.

We have treated the edge of our urban areas generally as a temporary boundary where, until the next development plan will rezone land outside the existing built up area, the current zoning forms a temporary development boundary to the town in question.

Most of all, we have avoided the thorny issue of 'contrasts' on which the vision outlined here, is based. Contrasts means differences between different parts of the country and this is generally difficult to accept politically. The tendency in our democratic decision-making system is that all parts of the country should receive the same treatment and this runs counter to the principle of contrast between different parts of the country.

One must also question the principle of Balanced Regional Development which is currently a core principle of the National Spatial Strategy and has been a core objective of government policy introduced in the National Development Plan. The objective includes policies to ease the pressure on urban infrastructure, to tackle urban and rural poverty and better integrate physical and economic planning. The objective of balanced regional development is implemented through infrastructural investment and the promotion of regional gateways (urban growth centres) that were subsequently designated in the National Spatial Strategy. Experience with the implementation of the NSS is that it is not only extremely difficult to achieve, it is also arguable that the disadvantages of concentrating development in the Greater Dublin Area are not evident, particularly if the concept of a polycentric city region based on the Dublin-Belfast corridor, is embraced.